D. Caroline Coile, Ph.D.

Australian Shepherds

Everything About Purchase, Care, Nutrition, Behavior, and Training

BARRON'S

CONTENTS

HISTORY OF THE AUSTRALIAN SHEPHERD

The origin of the Australian name for this quintessential American dog will almost certainly remain a mystery.

The sound of the whistle, the bleating of the sheep, the barking of the dog, the rumble of hoofbeats—this is the song of the Australian Shepherd. It is a song accompanied by a graceful dance of dog and sheep, orchestrated by the shepherd. It is a dance that is not only a thing of beauty, but a necessity of ranch life. It is a dance that has been performed for generations.

Early History

One of the most essential roles of dogs throughout history has been that of a helper with livestock. Some breeds specialized in guarding the stock from marauding predators, others in herding the stock, and some combined both talents. Even among the herding breeds, dogs specialized in working cattle or sheep, or in driving or gathering. Thousands of generations of selection produced dogs so perfectly suited for every type of herding situation that they have never been surpassed by modern technology.

When European settlers came to America they brought with them the livestock and stock-tending dogs of their native lands. These breeds probably included the English Shepherd, Dorset Blue Shag, Cumberland Sheepdog, and Smithfield Sheepdog from England, the Scottish Collie from Scotland, the Glenwherry Collie from Ireland, the Welsh Grey Sheepdog from Wales, the Bouvier des Flandres from France, as well as several breeds from Germany and Spain. Just as America was a melting pot for human immigrants, so the various breeds began to interbreed.

The Gold Rush

Most of the sheep and sheepdogs remained in the eastern parts of America, where conditions were not that different from those of Europe. Western America posed a very different situation, however. Here the land was harsh, intensely hot in the arid southern regions and bone-chillingly cold in the North. Settlers from Spain populated the southern and California coastal regions, and with them came their Spanish shepherd dogs. Still, their numbers were low and these breeds remained distinct from their counterparts back East. The situation might have remained except for one word: "Gold!"

The rush was on, and so was the genesis of the Australian Shepherd. Until that time the vast and rugged areas of the far western regions of America had attracted only the most adventurous of settlers, but with the advent of the Gold Rush, people flocked to California. Huge flocks of sheep were driven from the Midwest and Southwest, and shipped from the East and abroad. As the sheep population grew, so did the sheepdog population. The dogs reflected the nationalities of their people, so most of the midwestern and eastern sheepdogs were of British stock, whereas those from the

Southwest were of Spanish descent. Most of the imported sheep came from Australia, and many were accompanied by Australian stock-dogs, which were in turn derived from British stock. Australian herding dogs had already begun to be selected for their ability to work in much more rugged conditions than their European ancestors, and these conditions more closely resembled those of the American West.

The sheepherders of the time did not care about their dogs' ancestry or looks; they depended upon them for their livelihood and simply bred the best workers to the best work-ers. Gradually, a strain of dogs emerged that was adept at handling stock in all types of

Fame

Perhaps the most watched Aussie ever was Hyper Hank, who was invited to perform his amazing Frisbee feats during half-time of Super Bowl XII.

rough terrain through blinding storms, sweltering heat, and frigid cold. These dogs had to react instantly to movements of the sheep as well as the commands of their sheepherder, but also had to be able to act independently and think for themselves. So was born the Australian Shepherd.

Later History

Why would this breed that was born and bred on American soil be dubbed "Australian"? The answer to this remains a mystery. One popular theory holds that these dogs accompanied Basque sheepherders arriving from Australia and formed the nexus of the herding dogs of the American West. However, most of the Basque sheepherders who arrived during the nineteenth century did so by way of Latin America and Europe; by the time Basque immigrants arrived en masse from Australia in the early twentieth century, the Australian Shepherd had already been established. Thus, the secret of the Australian Shepherd's name goes beyond the Basque immigrants, and may lie with the Australian immigrants who arrived with their sheep and dogs in the mid 1800s. Perhaps their dogs had a distinctive look that set them apart from the other sheepherding dogs of the time. Some conjecture exists that the Australian imports may have included a large number of merle-colored animals, and

that people began to refer to any merle-colored shepherd as an Australian Shepherd.

Legend has it that the Native Americans of the West held these "ghost-eyed" dogs to be sacred, and avoided them and their people. Like its name, the origin and history of the Australian Shepherd will likely always be cloaked in doubt, but its uncanny ability to predict and control the movements of livestock, as well as capture the hearts of humans, might very well be evidence that the Native Americans were right.

The Australian Shepherd continued to prosper in the West, proving itself an invaluable ranch hand. These dogs had to be quick, hardy, obedient, intelligent, weatherproof, and tireless. Generations of selection for working ability produced the American West's preeminent sheepdog, yet it was still more of a strain or type than a breed. The dogs were relatively unknown outside of the West or off the ranch. The situation changed with a man named Jay Sisler, whose Aussies showed they could turn their intelligence and athleticism to other areas. They became hits as trick dogs in touring rodeos of the 1950s and 1960s. The big break came when they were given roles in several films, most notably the Disney films *Run Appaloosa Run* and *Stub: The Greatest Cowdog in the West.* So astounding were these dogs that moviegoers and dog fanciers who had never seen such feats or dogs traveled to the West to see them in action, often returning with one of their own. Many of today's Aussies can be traced back to Sisler's rodeo dogs.

Even before the Aussie found fame on the big screen, a few dog fanciers, mostly in the western United States, had discovered these impressive dogs. In 1957 they formed the Australian Shepherd Club of America (ASCA). In that same year the National Stock Dog Registry (NSDR) became the official registration body for the breed. The NSDR's influence continued to help ensure that the Aussie would remain a functional herding dog rather than a dog bred primarily for beauty. As the breed gained in popularity, however, more fanciers wanted to also enjoy competition in obedience and conformation forums, and in 1971 the ASCA took over as the official registry. Aussies registered with the ASCA could take part in a wide variety of competitive venues, making the Aussie more attractive to fanciers who were not in a position to train their dogs for herding trials. In 1977 a breed standard by which the conformation of Aussies could be objectively evaluated was approved (see pages 105–108). For some

Aussie fanciers, the next logical step was to seek American Kennel Club (AKC) recognition.

AKC Recognition

Not all breed fanciers wanted AKC recognition, however, so when it was proposed in 1985, the ASCA declined to pursue AKC affiliation. Many club members feared that the emphasis on conformation competition that often accompanies AKC recognition would divide the breed into show and herding types, rather than the all-purpose Aussie they valued. In addition, the increased popularity that is sometimes created by the words "AKC registered" was worrisome, as the Aussie was not a breed for everyone. Nonetheless, several Aussie breeders felt that AKC recognition would benefit the breed, and in 1991 they formed the United States Australian Shepherd Association (USASA). They modified the ASCA standard and petitioned the AKC for full recognition, which was granted in 1993. The situation has left the Australian Shepherd with two parent clubs in the United States: the original and largest is the ASCA; the official AKC club is the USASA.

The Aussie has since become a major contender in the herding group at AKC dog shows, and a strong competitor at AKC herding trials. It is still a valued working dog and staunch herding trial contender at non-AKC events. Despite an influx of fanciers interested primarily in show, the Aussie has kept its base of breeders who believe the Aussie should be, above all, a working stockdog with exceptional temperament.

The Aussie has continued to grow in popularity as a pet, but not always for the good of the dogs, their owners, or the breed as a whole.

Although the breed seems to have withstood many of the detrimental aspects of AKC recognition, the ASCA was definitely right about one thing: The Aussie is not the breed for everyone.

Temperament

As the Australian Shepherd finds its way into more and more homes, it is also finding its way into more unsuitable situations. Think carefully before asking an Aussie to share your life. Aussies are active dogs and will not understand why you have abandoned them to a pen in the yard, the garage, or the pound. Too often, prospective dog owners select their new dog based upon its physical characteristics, with the assumption that all dogs act alike. They do not. Generations of selection have seen to that. Behavior is malleable, but dogs are born with a propensity to act in certain ways dictated by their genes. Not all dogs within a breed act the same, but most dogs within a breed have a tendency to act in certain ways, especially if those traits are important ones for doing the job for which the breed was developed. Don't get an Aussie and expect it to act like a retriever—that's just not in its genes. And besides, to try to change the breed would be to deprive it of its heritage.

Genetic Heritage

So what is the Australian Shepherd's genetic heritage?

- ✔ The Aussie is an energetic, playful, intelligent, biddable dog that is happiest when it has a job to do.
- ✔ It can be a well-mannered and calm dog in the house as long as it is given adequate

exercise—mental and physical—throughout the day.

✔ It is a devoted companion, loving and loyal to its family.

✔ It has a protective nature, and will guard its family bravely.

✔ It is an excellent watchdog, and a pretty good protection dog. This is not a dog that will throw itself on strangers in greeting; instead, it is reserved with those it doesn't know. A few Aussies go beyond "reserved" and are instead shy with strangers.

✔ The Aussie generally gets along well with other dogs and pets.

Herding Tendencies

Herding is the breed's reason for being, and what truly defines the Aussie. This urge to herd is essential for people wanting an Aussie as a stockdog or herding competitor, but it can be an irritating trait to people looking for the traditional suburban pet. Lacking stock, these dogs will sometimes try to herd other pets (which may cause conflicts if the other pet becomes sufficiently annoyed) or children (which can scare those unfamiliar with the dog's behavior), and some have a tendency to chase moving vehicles. Sometimes the dog will nip at heels or grasp a hand in its mouth, causing some people to believe the dog is acting aggressively. Herding inappropriate objects is not a universal problem

Merle DNA Testing

GenMark offers a DNA test that can tell you if your Aussie has 0, 1, or 2 M genes for merle. For more information, go to *http://www.genmarkag.com/canine_faqs.php* or call them at 877-766-3446.

and it can be trained out if done early and consistently. After all, a good herding dog knows when and what to herd. Unlike many herding breeds, Aussies are not overly enthusiastic barkers. They will bark an alert if something seems amiss, and they may bark in play, but they do not (as a rule) bark incessantly unless they are bored and neglected. The key traits of the herding dogs are intelligence and energy. These are traits that seem good, but can be troublesome for pet owners.

Intelligence

The Aussie is uncannily intelligent. It has to be in order to learn and instantly respond to fairly complicated commands, as well as to think on its own in controlling stock. Most people think they want an intelligent dog, but very few people are prepared to deal with and nurture that intelligence. An intelligent child that is given no direction or stimulation is on its way to becoming a problem child; the same is true for an intelligent dog. If you plan to keep your dog in a crate a good part of the day, or even locked in the house alone while you work, then you don't want a dog whose mind is racing with ideas and a need for entertainment. You want a dull dog (actually, if you plan to ignore your dog you want a stuffed dog). An intelligent dog will look for ways to entertain itself and it will find them. It will dig, bark, get into the garbage, redecorate, escape, and come up with some amazingly mischievous ideas. Then what happens? Owners of such dogs try to remove all possible items the dog could entertain itself with, or lock the dog in a crate or run. The dog will always find a way to do something, even if it is only barking or biting itself—and when it finally gets a chance to do something, it is so crazed with relief that its owners consider it uncontrollable. They conclude that this supposedly intelligent breed is actually stupid and wild, and take it on a one-way trip to the dog pound. An intelligent dog needs intelligent things to do.

Energy Level

The Aussie is also a tireless athlete. Herding is not a short-term activity; the day of the working ranch dog is long and hard. The herding dog must be able to travel mile after mile, ever ready with short bursts of speed, hairpin turns, and skidding stops. Even when at a standstill it is ever vigilant, always on the alert for breaking stock, intruders, or its master's next command. Again, most people think they want an active dog, but far too often they

place that active dog in a crate or apartment and think a walk around the neighborhood will satisfy its needs. It will not. The Aussie needs to run long and hard. If not given the chance to expend its large energy reserves, it will try to do so inside the house. Then its owners become more and more irritated with the dog, finally label it as hyperactive, and take it to the dog pound. An active dog needs activity.

Make sure you understand the Aussie before inviting one into your home. You are the one that can read and do research; your future Aussie doesn't have that advantage. It is at the mercy of its breeder's and future owner's good sense and judgment. Your Aussie is simply doing what it has been selected to do for uncounted generations.

OBTAINING AN AUSTRALIAN SHEPHERD

The Aussie's heritage as a dog bred primarily for working ability rather than looks has resulted in a breed with a wide variety of different but equally correct types.

Authentic Aussies have several traits in common that are easy to discern as long as you know what to look for. The next step is knowing where to find one.

Finding an Aussie

Before embarking on your search for an Aussie, take a moment to clarify exactly what traits you feel are most important in your new dog. Most people insist upon good temperament, good health, and good looks. Some people also want promising herding, show, or obedience potential.

Good Temperament

More than owners of most breeds, Aussie owners list temperament as the top priority in selecting a breed. Most Aussies do have excellent temperaments, but you should still take some precautions when choosing your future partner.

The personality of the sire and dam are the best indicators of that of their offspring. The Aussie is naturally wary of and reserved with strangers, but it should not act afraid or aggressive. A dam with very young puppies may act protectively; if so, she should be revisited when the pups are a little older.

The presence of obedience or herding titles in the pedigree indicates not only obedient ancestors, but breeders who care about temperament. Aussies are talented obedience and herding competitors, so it is not unusual to find a pedigree chock full of title holders. Note that a dog from a strong herding background may not be the best choice for a sedentary lifestyle (but then, no Aussie is); however, it is strongly desirable if you wish to work stock. Many true working Aussies have no titleholders in their backgrounds; they are too busy pursuing stock to take time off to pursue titles. Your best evidence is to watch the parents or other relatives actually working stock on the ranch.

Equally important is the environment in which the puppy is raised. Pups raised with

Breeder's Directories

Start your search for a good breeder here:

- ASCA Breeders' directory: *http://www.asca.org/Finding+an+Aussie/Breeders+Directory*
- USASA Breeders' directory: *http://www.australianshepherds.org/directory.html*

minimal (or unpleasant) human contact during their critical period of development (from about six to ten weeks of age) may have some lifetime personality problems. Notice how the breeder interacts with the adults and pups, and whether the puppies are being raised under-foot (good) or out of sight (bad).

Good Health

Aussies are generally a healthy and hardy breed, commonly reaching the age of 12 or more. The chances of sharing a long life with your Aussie will be greatly increased if you carefully screen your source to ensure that your potential pup is as free as possible from hereditary problems. It may seem initially easier to run out and buy the first cute Aussie pup you find, but the effort you save will be incon-sequential compared to the time, expense, and grief you will encounter if that pup later develops a serious hereditary illness. No matter how much research you do into the back-ground of any puppy, there is no guarantee that your dog will live a long and healthy life, but why not go with the odds and choose a dog from the healthiest background possible?

Every pure breed of dog is a pure breed because it has only a subset of the genes avail-able to the entire canine population. Sometimes this subset of genes includes genes responsible for a disease. When genes for a particular disease are more common in one breed than in another, that breed is said to have a hereditary predispo-sition to that disease. The Australian Shepherd has hereditary predispositions to several health problems although none is overwhelming.

According to health surveys and the Aus-tralian Shepherd Health and Genetics Institute, the following problems are the most common in Aussies, in this order:

1. Cataracts: Cataracts, an opacity in the lens of the eye, in Aussies may be hereditary. The type seen in Aussies appears to be dominantly inherited, with incomplete penetrance, which means not all dogs will be affected to the same extent. Many dogs get cloudy lenses when they get old, but cataracts tend to be more opaque and come at an earlier age, often in Aussies as young as 18 months of age. Dogs with severe cataracts may need to have their lens replaced with an artificial one, just as is done for people. Screening is through yearly tests by a veterinary ophthalmologist, with clearance through the Canine Eye Registration Foundation (CERF).

2. Epilepsy: Epilepsy, which is basically repeated seizures of unknown origin, appears to be hereditary in several breeds, including Aussies. It's probably the problem of most concern to breeders because its effects are so frightening and disruptive. At this time, the genetic basis is unknown. No screening test is available. The first seizures are usually seen between 1.5 to 3 years of age. Not all seizures are caused by epilepsy, so any dog with a seizure should be thoroughly examined. Medication can help in many, but not all, cases.

3. Dental faults: Just as in people, Aussies can have poor occlusion, including overbites, underbites, and wry bites (where it's over on one side and under on the other). They also may have missing teeth. Unless severe, none of these dental problems cause any discomfort. You can see for yourself how the bite is in the parents of your puppy, and in the puppy himself.

4. Autoimmune disease: Autoimmune diseases are ones in which the immune system malfunctions and destroys parts of the dog's body as though those parts were foreign

Collie Eye Anomaly (CEA)

In CEA, several structures in the rear portion of the eye develop abnormally. These include the retina (part of the eye containing the light-sensitive cells), retinal blood vessels, tapetum (the reflective layer responsible for "eyeshine" at night), and the optic disk (place where the nerve from the eye to the brain leaves the eye). CEA varies greatly in severity between affected dogs; mild cases can result in a large blind spot, and more severe cases can result in retinal detachment and blindness.

CEA can be detected in pups as young as six to eight weeks of age, but does not get worse with age. In fact, it sometimes appears to improve (a phenomenon known as "go normal"), although this appearance is caused by other parts of the maturing eye obscuring small affected areas. According to CERF statistics, about 1 percent of Aussies have CEA, which is much less than it used to be.

intruders. In Aussies, they most often take the form of thyroiditis, lupus, and generalized demodectic mange. These problems seem to run in families, but no genetic mechanism is known.

5. Hip dysplasia (CHD): The bane of many large breeds, in CHD the ball of the femur (thigh) bone does not fit properly in the socket of the pelvic bone. Hip radiographs (X rays) can be diagnostic of dysplasia before outward signs of the disorder can be perceived. Radiographs are rated by either the Orthopedic Foundation for Animals (OFA) or the Pennsylvania Hip Improvement Program (PennHIP).

Current OFA statistics show that about 6 percent of Aussies in their records are dysplastic, and about 15 percent are rated "excellent."

This means that about about 80 percent have passable hips with "good" or "fair" ratings.

CHD has been shown to have a hereditary basis, but it is a complex disorder involving many factors. This means that it is possible that parents free of the condition can still produce dysplastic offspring, and dysplastic parents can produce clear offspring. On the whole, however, the chances are far greater of getting clear puppies from clear parents.

6. Coloboma: Colobomas refer to a failure of proper closure of fetal tissue, resulting in open pits in various structures of the eye.

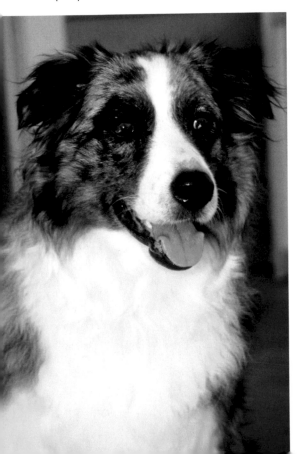

Colobomas of the retina or optic disk are often associated with CEA. Iris colobomas, which appear as openings in the colored portion of the eye, are more common in merle or predominantly white Aussies. Do not confuse iris colobomas with heterochromia, which is an iris of more than one color. Heterochromia is often seen in merles and is not considered a defect.

7. Allergies: Many dogs of all breeds, including Aussies, suffer from allergies, either to inhaled pollens or, less commonly, to food. Because some breeds are more affected than others, a genetic basis is suspected.

8. Cancer: Whenever cancer occurs in any breed, it's devastating. In Aussies, two types of deadly cancers, hemangiosarcoma and lymphoma, may be overrepresented. No screening tests are available, but you can ask the breeder about the cause of death in relatives.

9. Persistant pupilary membrane: Sometimes a small membrane is stretched across the pupil. It's supposed to go away before birth, and sometimes it still will go away by 6 months of age. If it persists, it doesn't usually cause any problems, but occasionally it can obscure vision. It would be noted in a CERF report.

10. Distichiasis: When one or more eyelashes are misdirected so they brush against the cornea of the eye, they can cause problems from discomfort to corneal ulcers. Surgery may be needed to correct the situation.

For more information of hereditary disorders in Aussies, go to *http://www.ashgi.org/articles/prevalance.htm*

Homozygous merle: Many people think of a merle-colored Aussie when they set out to find a puppy. They may naturally assume that the best way to get a merle puppy is to find a litter with two merle parents. Many inexperienced breeders also assume that the best way to get merles is to breed from two merle parents. This is a grave mistake.

The merle allele *(M)* is a dominant gene; only one copy of it is required in order to result in merle coloration. A dog with one copy of the *M* allele would be merle, and have the genotype *Mm* (so-called heterozygous merle). A dog with no *M* allele would not be merle, and would have the genotype *mm* (so-called homozygous non-merle.)The problem arises with a dog with two *M* alleles, having the genotype *MM* (so-called homozygous merle, or double merle.) The *M* allele is actually an incompletely dominant gene, because the presence of two *M* alleles does not result in merle, but instead in a predominantly white dog with spots of merle. Note that although most double merles are predominantly white, some double merles from lines that are naturally extremely dark may not appear to be markedly white compared to other Aussies, but have much more white than is typical for their line.

The *MM* genotype is associated with sensory defects in dogs. This is because the *MM* genotype also affects the presence of some pigment in the inner ear that is necessary for hearing; it also causes aberrant development of eye tissues. The extent of the problems varies between individuals. Double merles are often euthanized at birth; however, many double merles live full lives.

Note: White trim, such as that on the feet, tail tip, face, and collar, should not be confused with the white of double merles. This white trim pattern (called Irish marking) is due to a separate recessive gene at an entirely different location, and has no detrimental effects.

Don't be scared off by what may appear to be a long list of problems. The typical Australian Shepherd is healthy and free of hereditary disease—but don't be oblivious to these problems either.

CHIC Tests

The Canine Health Information Center (CHIC) is a repository of testing data. Rather than tests all breeds for the same thing, each breed club suggests the most relevant tests for their breeds. The tests suggested for Australian Shepherds are
- Hip dysplasia—OFA evaluation
- Elbow Dysplasia—OFA evaluation
- Eye Clearance—CERF evaluation
- Autoimmune thyroiditis (optional)—OFA evaluation from an approved laboratory
- Collie Eye Anomaly (Optional)—Optigen test results registered with the OFA
- Multiple drug sensitivity (optional)—Washington State University Veterinary Clinical Pharmacology Lab test results registered with the OFA—WSU VCPL. First-Generation Offspring of tested dogs eligible for clearance by their parentage.

Puppy Health Checklist

Your prospective puppy should:
- ✔ have its first vaccinations and deworming.
- ✔ be outgoing and active; avoid a puppy that shows signs of fearfulness or aggressiveness. If a pup is apathetic or sleepy, it could be that it just ate, but it could also be a sign of sickness.
- ✔ be clean, with no missing hair, crusted or reddened skin, or signs of parasites. Eyes, ears, and nose should be free of discharge.
- ✔ have pink gums; pale gums may indicate anemia.

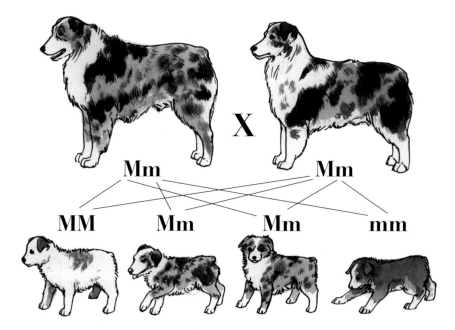

X

Mm   Mm

MM   Mm   Mm   mm

✔ have no indication of redness or irritation around the anus.
✔ not be coughing, sneezing, or vomiting.
✔ not be thin or pot-bellied.
✔ not be dehydrated, which can suggest repeated vomiting or diarrhea. Test for dehydration by picking up a fold of skin and releasing it. The skin should "pop" back into place.

Good Looks

You want your Aussie to look like an Aussie, which means it will need to have at the very least some of the more important Aussie characteristics. The Australian Shepherd is a medium-sized dog with a cobby, athletic build, slightly longer than tall. Its coat is of medium length and slightly coarse texture. It has a

A breeding of merle (Mm) to a merle (Mm) produces 50% merles (Mm), 25% non-merles (mm), and 25% homozygous merles (MM).

fairly broad head with a muzzle of approximately the same length as the backskull. Its ears are triangular, set on high, and fold forward. It usually has a bobtail. These traits are the basics of Aussie type; more exacting requirements are set forth in the Australian Shepherd standard of perfection (see The ASCA Standard, pages 105–108).

Conformity to the official standards also requires sound body structure. Soundness refers to the ability to move in an efficient manner so that your Aussie can run, herd, and play tirelessly. Unsound Aussies may have feet that point outward rather than forward, or may have legs that interfere with each other when trotting, or may have any number of structural faults that result in an inefficient stride. Soundness is a trait more vital to the show or working dog than to the pet. Even some great working dogs are not particularly sound by show standards but are certainly proven by performance.

The appearance of the sire and dam of the litter is the best indication of the looks of their offspring. Good breeders will have photos of the entire family available. By examining the pedigree for conformation champions, you can also get an idea of how well your dog's ancestors conform to the official standards.

Custom Choices

Finally, the fun part—deciding what color, sex, and age Aussie is best suited for you. These choices are all just part of personal preferences; you really can't go wrong (with one exception: the double merle).

Colors

Aussies come in what seems to be an amazing array of colors, but the diversity can be explained by the interactions of four main color choices:

✔ black vs. liver
✔ merle vs. non-merle
✔ self vs. tan-pointed
✔ solid vs. white trimmed

Aussies can have either a black or brown (liver) base color. The black is due to a dominant allele *(B)*, and the brown is due to a recessive allele *(b)*. A dog with two *b* alleles will have no black pigment on its body, which means that the nose and eye rims (which are usually black in black Aussies), will be liver-colored. The eyes also tend to be lighter colored.

The inheritance of merle is illustrated on page 18. Merles and non-merles are equally correct and equally healthy, although merles are prone to a few more minor eye problems. Phantom merles are merles with such small areas of dilute pigment that they may appear to be non-merles. Double merles result in Aussies that are predominantly white and that may be unhealthy. Do not get a predominantly white Aussie!

All colors and patterns can either be self (meaning distributed over all the dark areas of the body) or tan-pointed (also called copper trim), where the eyebrows, cheeks, and inner legs are tan. In addition, all colors and patterns can be either without any white or with Irish marking, in which the lower legs, tail tip, muzzle, and collar are white.

Tails

Adult Aussies traditionally have very short tails, but not all of them are born that way; some are "natural bobs" that require no docking. It might seem that a natural bob is preferable but some evidence exists that dogs with naturally short tails are more prone to congenital spinal defects. In fact, natural bobs should never be bred to each other because their offspring are more likely to have spinal defects. Puppies usually have their tails docked within

Breeder Checklist

Responsible breeders:
- ✔ breed only one or two breeds of dogs, so they can concentrate on just those breeds.
- ✔ breed no more than three or four litters per year, so they can concentrate on those litters.
- ✔ can compare their dogs objectively to the Aussie standard.
- ✔ can discuss Aussie health concerns and provide evidence of the health of their own dogs.
- ✔ can give substantial reasons relating to quality of conformation, performance, and health why they bred the litters or chose those parents.
- ✔ have pictures of several generations of the puppy's ancestors.
- ✔ have clean, friendly, healthy adults.
- ✔ have clean facilities that promote interaction with their dogs.
- ✔ raise their litters inside the house and underfoot, not in a kennel or garage.
- ✔ question you about your facilities, your prior experiences with dogs, and your intentions regarding your new dog.
- ✔ sell companion-quality puppies only with limited registration, which means their progeny cannot be registered.
- ✔ insist upon taking the dog back should you be unable to keep it at any time during its life.

the first few days of life, either by a tight ligature that prevents blood from circulating in the tail so that it dies and falls off, or by cutting it off. Either way, many breeders contend that little or no pain is involved. In fact, research has shown that some pain likely is involved, but the extent of it cannot be measured.

Why dock tails? The tradition may have arisen because the first Aussies worked in areas full of briars that could become enmeshed in the tail hair. In addition, the wagging tail can become bloodied by hitting against briars and rocks. Undocked tails with long hair are more prone to hygiene problems due to fecal matter, and shepherds may have docked their dogs' tails for this reason, just as they did their sheep's tails. Even if you object to the idea of your pup's tail being docked, you will be hard pressed to convince a breeder to leave a pup undocked for you. If you changed your mind about getting the pup it would be difficult to place, and docking the tail of an older dog is definitely painful. Note, however, that in several European countries docking is illegal, so that unless they are natural bobtails Aussies often have long tails.

Male or Female?

Aussie males are larger (20 to 23 inches [51 to 58 cm] at the shoulder and from 50 to 65 pounds [23 to 29 kg]) and have longer coats, heavier bones, and larger heads than females. Females are about 18 to 21 inches (46 to 53 cm) tall and from 35 to 50 pounds (16 to 23 kg). Males tend to be somewhat prouder and more territorial; the drawback is they don't always get along well with other males. Males are also apt to go off in search of females, and often think nothing of repeatedly lifting their leg on your furniture to mark your house as their territory. On the other hand, females come in estrus ("season" or "heat") twice a year; this lasts for three weeks, during which time you must keep your female away from amorous neighborhood males who consider your house a singles bar. You must also contend with her bloody discharge and possible attempts to elope with her suitors. The solution for both sexes is neutering (see page 56).

Puppy or Adult?

The easiest time for puppies to change homes is between eight and twelve weeks of age, but if you definitely want a competition-quality dog you may have to wait until the pup is five or six months old. An adult Aussie may need a longer adjustment period. No matter what the age, if the puppy has been properly socialized (that is, treated gently and exposed to a variety of situations, people, and dogs), your Aussie will soon blend into your family life and love you as though it's always owned you. If you want to work stock with your dog, then you will want it to be introduced to nonthreatening stock, such as ducks, at a young age.

Puppies are not for everyone. No one can deny that a puppy is cute and fun, but a puppy is much like a baby; you can't ever be too busy to walk, feed, supervise, or clean (and clean and clean). If you work away from home, have limited patience, or heirloom rugs, an older puppy or adult may be a better choice. Young Aussie pups are actually fairly obedient, but if you think an adult Aussie is active, you haven't seen anything until you've seen a youngster in action.

Breeders may have older retired dogs available that would relish the chance to live as a pampered pet. Several rescue groups are devoted to finding homes for Aussies in need of loving homes (see listings on page 109). In most cases their only crime was the misfortune of being placed with uninformed owners.

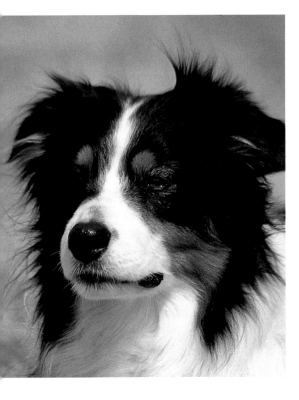

mation champions. Those destined for stock work should have a strong desire to herd—they should have the promise of becoming dependable helpers with stock. Many Aussies are able to compete successfully in herding, obedience, and conformation.

Breeding-quality dogs come from impeccable backgrounds, and are of even higher quality than are competition-quality dogs. Breeding quality means more than the ability to impregnate or conceive, but far too often these are the only criteria applied to prospective parents by owners unduly impressed by a registration certificate. It is difficult to pick a competition-quality puppy at an early age; it is impossible to pick a breeding-quality puppy.

The better quality you demand, the longer your search will take. A couple of months is a reasonable time to look for a pet puppy, a couple of years for a breeding-quality dog. Begin your search for a high-quality Aussie by seeing as many Aussies as possible, talking to Aussie breeders, attending Aussie competitions, joining an Aussie Internet newsgroup, and reading every available Aussie publication.

Quality

Dogs are generally graded as pet, competition or working, and breeding quality.

A pet-quality dog is one that has some trait that would prevent it from winning in conformation, herding, or perhaps obedience competition, but still has good health and temperament. Being a pet is the most important role a dog can fulfill, and pet quality should never be belittled.

Competition- or working-quality dogs should first of all be pet quality; that is, they should have good temperament and health. Those destined for the show ring should portray the attributes called for in the breed standard so that they could be expected to become confor-

AKC or ASCA Registration

In most breeds the decision regarding registration is simple: AKC-registered versus not registered at all. In Aussies the decisions regarding registration are far more complex.

The reason traces back to the dispute over the Aussie's future as a show versus a working dog. When the AKC began registering Australian Shepherds, many concerned breeders declined to register their stock because they feared AKC recognition would encourage overbreeding or breeding for only cosmetic traits; thus, while

Rescue

Responsible breeders provide a home for the dogs they breed for life should their new owners not be able to keep them. But not all Aussies are bred by responsible breeders, and even responsible breeders sometimes have unforeseen circumstances and can't take back a dog.

Aussies end up in rescue for many reasons. Some owners find their dogs demand too much of their time, or consider the Aussie's energy level too much to live with. Some owners find their dogs have medical conditions they're not willing or able to pay for. Some owners die, some have unforeseen circumstances, and some simply tire of having a dog. Some were used as breeding stock in puppy mills and have been discarded because they're past their prime. Whatever the reason, rescue Aussies are filled with love but have no one on whom to lavish it. Occasionally they have behavior problems, often stemming from poor training or socialization, but good rescue organizations will make sure you know any problems ahead of time and will help you guide your Aussie to becoming the best dog he can be. Rescue Aussies range from the occasional puppy to the more common middle-aged or senior dog, but they all have in common a need for a forever home they can call their own. See page 109 for a list of Aussie Rescue groups.

some great Aussies are AKC-registered, many equally beautiful purebred Aussies are instead registered with the Australian Shepherd Club of America (ASCA). In fact, the ASCA is not only the traditional registering body for Aussies, but the largest, with more than 150,000 Aussies

registered. Those Aussie breeders who have interest only in stockwork prefer to register their dogs with the International English Shepherd Registry (IESR), also known as the National Stock Dog Registry (NSDR).

If you are not particularly interested in breeding or competing with your Aussie, the registering body will not be of primary importance. If you wish to compete with your dog, however, bear in mind that to compete in AKC events a dog must be AKC-registered, and to compete in ASCA events a dog must be ASCA-registered. Many Aussies are registered with both AKC and ASCA.

Even if you have no intention of competing with your Aussie, the type of registry can be an important factor. If you want to use your Aussie to work stock, you would be better served to choose an Aussie from a strong herding background, such as those registered with the ASCA or NSDR. The downside is that such dogs may be even more energetic than dogs from nonworking backgrounds, and energetic dogs can be a handful unless you give them a job to do. If you want your Aussie to look like the one you saw winning at a dog show, your best bet is to get an AKC- or ASCA-registered dog from a show line.

Nonregistered dogs make great pets; however, they are not eligible for conformation competition, and may be eligible for other AKC or ASCA performance competitions only upon applying for a special type of registration allowing for limited types of competition.

A final note of caution: Registered puppies should come with a pedigree and either a litter registration certificate, individual registration certificate, or statement in writing clearly stating why such documents are not being supplied.

AUSTRALIAN SHEPHERDS AS HOUSE PETS

The Aussie has always expected to be a real member of the family, sharing family activities and, of course, the family home.

In turn, Aussie owners expect their charges to act civilized, not using the antique furniture as a chewbone or the heirloom rugs as a bathroom.

Your Aussie now faces the transition from canine litter member to human family member. Every day will be full of novel experiences and new rules. Your pup is naturally inquisitive and will need you to guide him toward becoming a well-mannered member of the household.

Half the excitement of welcoming a new dog is preparing for the big homecoming. Puppy-proofing your home will be a lot easier if you do it before your new puppy is underfoot, undoing everything as fast as you can do it. Much of the fun comes from an Aussie accessory buying spree. The best sources for supplies are large pet stores, dog shows, and discount pet catalogs.

Accessories for Aussies

Consider the following supplies:

✔ Buckle collar: for wearing around the house; avoid leather, which can stain the coat. A wide, soft collar is more comfortable for the dog than a narrow stiff collar.

✔ Nylon choke or martingale collar: safer for walking on lead, never to be left on the dog!

✔ Leash: nylon, web, or leather—never chain. An adjustable show lead is good for puppies.

✔ Lightweight retractable leash: better for older adults; be sure not to drop the leash as it can retract toward the pup and frighten it.

✔ Stainless steel food and water bowls: avoid plastic, which can cause allergic reactions and retain germs.

✔ Crate: large enough for an adult Aussie to stand up in without having to lower its head. You may need to divide it so that the available space for a puppy is smaller (see page 28).

✔ Exercise pen: tall enough that an adult Aussie can't jump over, or preferably with a top (see page 28 for a description).

✔ Toys: fleece-type toys, ball, stuffed animals, stuffed socks, empty plastic milk or soda bottles. Make sure no parts of toys can be pulled off and swallowed.

✔ Chewbones: the equivalent of a teething ring for babies. Avoid rawhide.

✔ Anti-chew preparations, such as Bitter Apple: The unpleasant taste discourages pups from chewing on items sprayed with it.

✔ Baby gate(s): better than a shut door for placing parts of your home off-limits. Do not use the accordion-style gates, in which a dog can get its head stuck and be asphyxiated.

✔ Soft brush.

✔ Nail clippers: Guillotine type is easier to use.

✔ Poop scoop: Two-piece rake type is best for grass.

✔ Dog shampoo (see page 64 for choices).

✔ First aid kit (see page 69 for contents).

✔ Food: start with the same food the pup is currently eating.

✔ Dog bed: a round cushion is heavenly, but you can also use the bottom of a plastic crate, or simply use an entire crate.

Safety Measures

Your puppy will naturally want to explore every nook and cranny of your house. Part of the pup's exploratory tools are its teeth, and any chewed items left in its wake are your fault, not your pup's—you are the one who should have known better—therefore, do not lash out at your pup. Give your pup a tap on the nose along with a firm *"No,"* and remove the item. If you come across one of your cherished items chewed to bits and feel compelled to lash out, go ahead—hit yourself in the head a few times for slipping up. It may teach you a lesson!

Any place your Aussie may wander must be Aussie-proofed. The first step is to do everything you would do to baby-proof your home. Get down at puppy level and see what dangers beckon.

Potential Killers

✔ drugs

✔ chocolate (especially baker's chocolate)

✔ rodent, snail, and insect baits

✔ antifreeze

✔ household cleaners

✔ paint thinner

✔ toilet fresheners

✔ nuts, bolts, pennies, which can dissolve in the stomach and cause zinc toxicity

✔ pins and needles, and anything in a sewing basket

✔ chicken bones or any bone that could be swallowed or could splinter

✔ sponges and sponge rubber balls

✔ any other small items that a pup could swallow, which can cause intestinal blockage

Puppy Proofing

Fill in the following checklist:

Check all over for
- ✔ uncovered electrical outlets
- ✔ open stairways, decks, or balconies
- ✔ unsecured doors

Check the kitchen for
- ✔ open cabinets holding cleaners and degreasers
- ✔ accessible garbage pails holding enticing rancid food and splintering bones
- ✔ pan handles extending invitingly over stovetop edges
- ✔ plastic wraps that can be lodged in the intestines

Check the dining room for
- ✔ hanging table cloths that, if pulled, can bring dishes crashing down
- ✔ swinging doors that can trap a puppy's head and neck

Check the family room for
- ✔ fireplace without a secure fire screen
- ✔ unsteady bookcases
- ✔ craft or sewing kits
- ✔ heavy statues or vases

Check the bedrooms for
- ✔ children's toys
- ✔ open closets, especially shoe closets

Check the bathrooms for
- ✔ pills and medicines
- ✔ hair treatments
- ✔ drain cleaners
- ✔ toilets with open lids
- ✔ razors
- ✔ diaper pails

Check the garage for
- ✔ antifreeze
- ✔ fuels, cleaners, paints—just about anything in a can
- ✔ batteries
- ✔ nails and screws
- ✔ herbicides, insecticides, and fertilizers
- ✔ rodent bait

Check the yard for
- ✔ weak fence
- ✔ rotted limbs
- ✔ unfenced pool
- ✔ cocoa mulch
- ✔ nut trees
- ✔ pointed sticks at eye level
- ✔ predators
- ✔ treated lawns
- ✔ poisonous plants
- ✔ insect hives

Housing

Before bringing your puppy home you should decide what parts of your home will be off-limits. Make sure that every family member understands the rules, and that they understand that sneaking the puppy onto off-limit furniture, for example, is not doing the puppy any favor at all. Like all dogs, Aussies enjoy the comfort of your chairs and sofas, but if you don't want them on the furniture, keep them off from the beginning. Don't pick the pup up to sit on your lap; instead, sit on the floor with him. Never fling the pup off furniture, or use mousetraps on furniture surfaces; both practices are dangerous and a terrible idea unless you like emergency visits to the veterinarian. There are several more humane items (available through pet catalogs) that emit a loud tone when a dog jumps on furniture, but these should not be necessary if you train your young puppy gently and consistently from the beginning.

The Kennel

A secure kennel run can be a convenient asset. It should be at least 6 feet (1.8 m) high and preferably have a top. Dogs can get more exercise in a long, narrow run as opposed to a square run of equal area. It should also have both shade and shelter. Dirt flooring can become muddy and harbor germs, as well as encourage digging. Cement flooring is easier to clean but is expensive. The best compromise flooring is probably pea gravel, which is fairly easy to keep clean. Beware—too fine a texture may cling to the dog's coat. The run can provide a secure area for your Aussie when you are away from home, but is not a substitute for a yard or a home.

The Crate

Many new dog owners are initially appalled at the idea of putting their pet in a crate as though he were some wild beast. At times, though, your Aussie pup can seem to be a wild beast, and a crate is one way to save your home from ruination and yourself from insanity. A crate can also provide a quiet haven for your youngster. Just as you hopefully find peace and security as you sink into your own bed at night, your pup needs a place that he can call his own, a place he can seek out whenever the need for rest and solitude arises. Used properly, your Aussie will come to think of his crate not as a way to keep himself in, but as a way to keep others out!

Don't expect your dog to stay in a crate all day, every day, while you are at work. Overuse of the crate is not only unfair, and even cruel, to the dog, but can also lead to behavior problems. An Aussie is an intelligent, active dog. To lock one in a crate without stimulation can result in such frustration and anxiety that the dog can begin to resent the crate and act uncontrollably when out of the crate. A crate should be the canine equivalent of a toddler's crib. It is a place for naptime, a place where you can leave your pup without worry of his hurting himself or your home. It is not a place for punishment, nor is it a storage box for your dog when you're through playing with him. Rethink getting an Aussie (or any dog) if you plan for him to live in a crate.

Nonetheless, the crate has its place in training. Place the crate in a corner of a quiet room, but not too far from the rest of the family. Put the pup in the crate when he begins to fall asleep, and he will become accustomed to using it as his bed. Be sure to place a soft blanket on the bottom. Also, by taking the pup directly from the crate to the outdoors upon awakening, the crate will be one of the handiest housebreaking aids at your disposal.

The X-pen

An exercise pen (or "X-pen") fulfills many of the same functions as a crate. X-pens are transportable wire folding "playpens" for dogs, typically about 4 feet by 4 feet (1.2 m × 1.2 m). X-pens are a reasonable solution when you must be away from home for a long time, because the pup can relieve himself on paper in one corner, sleep on a soft bed in the other, and frolic with his toys all over. It's like having a little yard inside the home. The X-pen also provides a safe time-out area when you just need some quiet time for yourself, but before leaving your pup in an X-pen, make sure that he cannot jump or climb out. Covers are available for incorrigible escapees. If you use an X-pen, cover the floor beneath it with thick plastic (an old shower curtain works well—unless he decides to attack it!), and then add towels or washable rugs for traction and absorbency. Again, do not expect to stick your Aussie in an X-pen all day every day and still have a sane dog.

Fencing

The number one Aussie accessory and lifesaver is a securely fenced yard. In today's world of automobiles and suburbs, a loose dog is at best an unwelcome visitor and, more often, a dead dog. Aussies can be gifted jumpers, climbers, diggers, and wrigglers, and are often tempted by the greener grass on the other side of the fence. Running stray dogs, playing children, racing bicycles, or just the call of the wild may prove irresistible to your dog.

Don't make the mistake many new owners make of testing their less-than-perfect fence to see if it just might work after all. Many dogs are actually inadvertently taught to be gifted escape artists by such situations. When the Aussie hops over the short fence, he has learned a very bad lesson. Even if the owner now adds an extension to raise the fence, the dog now has the jumping idea firmly implanted in his repertoire, and will likely test the new fence. If that one, too, can be jumped, the owner is in for a problem. If you want your Aussie to stay in the yard, make your yard escape-proof from the beginning. Adding progressive fixes only teaches your dog to escape little by little, just as you would gradually make

things tougher if you were purposefully teaching your dog to find a way out.

Invisible fences have become a popular alternative to traditional fences, but they do have some shortcomings. Because they only work with a dog that is wearing a special shock collar that is activated by the buried boundary wire, they can't keep out stray dogs that aren't wearing such a collar, nor can they keep out unscrupulous dognappers. In addition, an excited, determined, or fast-moving Aussie can be over the boundary before he has a chance to stop, and then find himself blocked out of the yard. Nonetheless, most owners report good results with these fences.

Never tie your dog out. It is cruel and dumb and is the perfect recipe for creating an aggressive, neurotic, unhappy dog—plus, your Aussie can choke to death, hurt his neck, or be attacked by strays.

Housebreaking

Aussies are easy to housebreak; still, most people have unrealistic expectations of their dog's ability to become housebroken, based in part upon friends boasting about their little genius that was housebroken at two weeks of age or something similarly ludicrous. No matter how wonderful and smart your Aussie is, he probably will not have full control over his elimination until he is around six months old, and may not be reliably housebroken until a year old. Be aware of the following blunders in housebreaking:

1. The number one housebreaking mistake made by most puppy owners is to give their puppies too much unsupervised freedom in the house. All canines have a natural desire to avoid soiling their denning area. The den area is considerably smaller than your entire house, however, and it will take some training before your pup extends the notion of den to your home.

You can use your dog's crate as his den, but if the crate is too large, the puppy may simply step away from the area he sleeps in and relieve himself at the other end of the crate. An overly large crate can be divided with a secure barrier until the puppy is larger or housebroken. Even so, your puppy may step just outside the door of the crate and eliminate there, because to the pup, that fulfills the natural requirement of not eliminating in the den. The puppy has failed to realize that he has just soiled *your* den, and the more the pup soils in a particular spot, the more he is likely to return to that same spot.

2. The second big mistake puppy owners make is to allow accidents to happen. Puppies have very weak control over their bowels, so if you don't take them to their elimination area often, they may not be able to avoid soiling. Puppies, like babies, have to eliminate a lot. You can't just stick them in a crate all day while you are at work and think you won't return home to a messy crate and messy pup. A rule of thumb is that a puppy can, at most, hold its bowels for as many hours as the pup is months old. This means that a three-month-old can hold himself for three hours. If the pup is forced to stay in a crate longer, so that he can't hold himself and has to soil the crate, you are setting the stage for a big problem. Once they get used to eliminating in their crate, they may continue.

Puppies tend to relieve themselves in areas that smell like urine. This is why it is so critical to never let the pup have an accident indoors; if he does, clean and deodorize the spot thoroughly and block the pup's access to that area. Use a pet deodorizer cleaner, and never use one containing ammonia—ammonia is a component of urine, so using an ammonia cleaner is like posting a sign that says "Go here!"

If you cannot be with your puppy for an extended period, you may wish to leave him outside (only in good weather and with cover) so that he will not be forced to have an indoor accident. If this is not possible, you may have to paper-train your puppy. Place newspapers on the far side of the room (or X-pen), away from the puppy's bed or water bowl; near a door to the outside is best. Place the puppy on the papers as soon as he starts to relieve himself.

A better option is to use sod squares instead of newspapers. Place the sod on a plastic sheet, and when soiled, take it outside and hose it off or replace it. By using sod, you are training the pup to relieve himself on the same surface he should eventually use outside. Place the soiled squares outside in the area you want your dog to use.

Because dogs are creatures of habit, housebreaking is more a matter of prevention than correction. To avoid accidents, learn to predict when your puppy will have to relieve himself. Immediately after awakening, and soon after heavy drinking or playing, your puppy will urinate. You will probably have to carry a younger baby outside to get him to the toilet area on time. Right after eating, or if nervous, your puppy will have to defecate. Circling, whining, sniffing, and generally acting worried usually signal that defecation is imminent. Even if the puppy starts to relieve himself, quickly but calmly scoop the pup up and carry him outside (the surprise of being picked up will usually cause the puppy to stop in midstream, so to speak). You can also clap your hands or make a loud noise to startle the pup so that he stops. You can add a firm *"No,"* but yelling and swatting are actually detrimental. When the puppy does relieve himself in his outside toilet, remember to heap on the praise and let your Aussie pup know how pleased you are. Adding a food treat really gets the point across. Keep some in a jar near the door and always accompany your pup outside so that you can reward him.

3. The number three housebreaking mistake made by dog owners is overuse of punishment. Even if you catch your dog in the act, overly enthusiastic correction tends only to teach the dog not to relieve himself in your presence, even when outside. This is why you should reward with a tidbit when the pup does relieve himself outside. Punishment doesn't make clear what is desired behavior, but reward makes it clear very quickly. Punishing a dog for a mess he has made earlier is totally fruitless; it only succeeds in convincing the dog that every once in a while, for no apparent reason, you are apt to go insane and attack him. It is a perfect recipe for ruining a trusting relationship. That "guilty" look you may think your dog is exhibiting is really fear that you have once again lost your mind.

4. The number four housebreaking mistake owners make is to open the door and push the pup outside by himself. After five minutes, the pup is let back in and promptly relieves himself on the rug. Bad dog? No, bad owner. Chances are the pup spent his time outside trying to get back inside to his owner. Puppies do not like to be alone, and knowing you are on the other side tdoors unappealing. In

ably huddled against
it when it was again
must go outside with
Don't take him for a walk,
play with him, simply go with him to his relief area, say *"Hurry up"* (the most popular choice of command words), and be ready to praise and perhaps give a treat when the pup does his deed. Then you can go to his play area or back inside.

As soon as you are hopeful your precocious puppy is housebroken, he will take a giant step backward and convince you there is no link between his brain and bowels. If your previously housebroken adult Aussie soils the house, it could be due to a physical or emotional problem. A physical examination is warranted any time a formerly housebroken dog begins to soil the house. You and your veterinarian will need to consider the following possibilities:

✔ Older dogs may simply not have the bladder control that they had as youngsters; a doggy door is the best solution.

✔ Older spayed females may "dribble"; ask your veterinarian about drug therapies.

✔ Several small urine spots (especially if bloody or dark) may indicate a bladder infection, which can cause a dog to urinate frequently.

✔ Sometimes a housebroken dog will be forced to soil the house because of a bout of diarrhea, and afterwards will continue to soil in the same area. If this happens, restrict that area from the dog, deodorize the area with an enzymatic cleaner, and revert to basic housebreaking lessons.

✔ Male dogs may "lift their leg" inside the house as a means of marking it as theirs. Castration will often solve this problem as long as it is

performed before the habit has become established; otherwise, diligent deodorizing and the use of some dog-deterring odorants (available at pet stores) may help.

✔ Submissive dogs, especially young females, may urinate upon greeting you; punishment only makes this "submissive urination" worse. For these dogs, be careful not to bend over or otherwise dominate the dog and to keep greetings calm. Submissive urination is usually outgrown as the dog gains more confidence.

✔ Some dogs defecate or urinate due to the stress of separation anxiety; you must treat the anxiety to cure the symptom. Dogs that mess their crate when left in it are usually suffering from separation anxiety or anxiety about being closed in a crate. Other telltale signs of anxiety-produced elimination are drooling, scratching, and escape-oriented behavior. You need to treat separation anxiety (see page 33) and start crate training again, placing the pup in it for a short period of time and working up gradually to longer times. Dogs that suffer from crate anxiety but not separation anxiety do better if left loose in a dog-proofed room.

Behavior Problems

No Aussie could really be awful, but even the best dogs with the best owners can sometimes do the worst things. Too often distraught owners get their training advice from the next-door neighbor or even dog trainers who don't have a scientific background in dog behavior analysis. Great strides have been made in recent years in canine behavioral therapy, so, if you're having a serious problem with your pet, before despairing, consult a certified canine behaviorist, who may employ a combination of conditioning and drug therapy to achieve a cure. Veterinarians can sometimes offer advice, but few are extensively trained in behavior. As a first step in any serious behavior problem, a thorough veterinary exam should be performed.

Sometimes the owner inadvertently makes the behavior worse, often through the overuse of punishment. If punishment doesn't work the first time, why do owners think that it will work the second, third, or fourth time? As the misbehavior continues in the face of punishment, the owners lay the blame on the dog. Inability to deal with what seems like inexcusable behavior too often leads the Aussie to the animal shelter.

Home Destruction

One of the most common canine behavior problems is home redecoration. Owners too often assume that the dog is angry at being left alone, and seeks to spite the owner by venting his rage on the home and its contents. Owners who continue to believe this erroneous idea never cure their dogs. Remember: Dogs never destroy out of spite.

Separation anxiety: The problem for many Aussies arises when their people leave them all alone. Being left alone is an extremely stressful situation for highly social animals. They react by becoming agitated and trying to escape from confinement. The telltale signature of a dog suffering from separation anxiety is that most of their destructive behavior is focused around doors and windows. Punishing the dog is ineffective because it actually *increases* the anxiety level of the dog as he comes to both look forward to and dread his owner's return.

The proper therapy is treatment of the dog's fear of being left alone. This is done by leaving the dog alone for very short periods of time and gradually working up to longer periods, taking care to never allow the dog to become anxious during any session. When you *must* leave the dog for long periods during the conditioning program, leave him in a different part of the house than the one in which the conditioning sessions take place.

When you return home, refrain from a joyous reunion scene. No matter what the condition of the home, greet the dog calmly or even ignore him for a few minutes, to emphasize the point that being left was really no big deal. Then have the dog perform a simple trick or obedience exercise so that you have an excuse to praise him. It takes a lot of patience, and often a whole lot of self-control, but it's not fair to you or your dog to let this situation continue.

Frustration or boredom: Not all home destruction arises from separation anxiety. Puppies are natural demolition dogs. The best cure (besides adulthood) is supervision. Adult Aussies still may destroy items through frustration or boredom. The best way to deal with these dogs is to provide both physical interaction (such as chasing a ball) and mental interaction (such as practicing a few simple obedience commands) an hour or so before leaving your dog. Several interactive toys are available that can provide hours of entertainment.

Fearfulness

The cardinal rule of working with a fearful dog is to never push him into situations that might overwhelm him.

Although usually happy to meet new friends, Aussies can be a bit cautious about strangers. Never force a dog that is afraid of people to be petted by somebody he doesn't know; it in no way helps the dog overcome his fear and is a good way for the stranger to get bitten. Strangers should be asked to ignore shy dogs, even when approached by the dog. Dogs seem to fear the attention of a stranger more than they fear the strangers themselves. When the dog gets braver, have the stranger offer him a tidbit, at first while not even looking at the dog. Gradual desensitization is time-consuming, but the best way to alleviate any fear.

Fear of thunder is a common problem in older dogs. Try to avoid it by acting cheerful when a thunderstorm strikes, and play with your dog or give him a tidbit. Once a dog develops a thunder phobia, try to find a recording of a thunderstorm, then play it at a very low level and reward your dog for calm behavior. Gradually increase the intensity and duration of the recording.

Never coddle your Aussie when he acts afraid, because it reinforces the behavior. It is always useful if your Aussie knows a few simple commands; performing these exercises correctly gives you a reason to praise the dog and also increases the dog's sense of security because he knows what is expected of him. For all causes of fear, the concept is the same: Never hurry, and never push the dog to the point that he is afraid.

Aggression

Many people erroneously believe that Aussies are being aggressive when they try to herd children, especially when nipping or grasping is involved, but this is more likely to be due to their herding instinct. Nonetheless, it can be unnerving. To dissuade an Aussie from acting in this manner, start young. True, it may seem cute in a puppy, but it will not be cute in an adult. First, try to prevent children from tempting the puppy with too much rambunctious behavior. If the dog does chase a child, the child should be instructed to stop, turn sideways to the dog with arms folded, and say *"No"* firmly. At the same time you can throw a can with some pennies in it (not *at* the dog!) so the rattling disrupts the dog's behavior, or give the dog a spritz of water from a water pistol.

Some dogs are afraid of children, either because they don't understand what they are or because they have had bad experiences with them. Introduce dogs and children to each other carefully, encouraging the child to be gentle and to offer the dog a treat. Unlike in humans, where direct eye contact is seen as a sign of sincerity, staring a dog directly in the eye is interpreted by the dog as a threat. It can cause a fearful dog to bite. Teach children not to stare at a strange dog.

Barking

The surest way to make your neighbors dislike your dog is to let him bark unchecked. Allow your Aussie to bark momentarily at strangers, and then call him to you and praise him for quiet behavior, distracting him with an obedience exercise if need be.

Isolated dogs will often bark through frustration or as a means of getting attention and alleviating loneliness. Even if the attention gained includes punishment, the dog will continue to bark in order to obtain the temporary presence of the owner. The simplest solution is to move the dog's quarters to a less isolated location. The distraction of a special chew toy, given only at bedtime, may help alleviate barking. In more stubborn cases, the use of collars

Guidelines for Good Behavior

✔ Harsh corrections only make matters worse.

✔ Dogs live in the present and cannot make the connection between their earlier misdeeds and later punishment.

✔ Dogs repeat actions that bring immediate rewards.

✔ Dogs don't understand the concept of making an exception "just this once."

✔ Dogs hear what you say, not what you mean to say. Be consistent with commands.

that emit a whiff of citronella whenever the dog barks have proved effective. The pup that must spend the day home alone is a greater challenge. Again, the simplest solution is to change the situation—a good excuse to get two Aussies!

Body language: (a) confident posture (yawning, panting, drooling, or slinking would indicate lack of confidence); (b) extremely submissive posture (ears back, body lowered, head averted); (c) dominant, aggressive posture (upright and stiff stance, direct stare, raised hackles); (d) playful posture (wagging rear end or tail, lowered front, opened mouth).

TRAINING AUSTRALIAN SHEPHERDS

Use the methods the professionals use, and you will be astounded by what your Aussie can learn.

Your Aussie will need some guidance in order to be a civilized member of society. You have an advantage, however—Aussies, especially young Aussies, are natural followers, not leaders. Your Aussie will elect you as his leader, and will expect you to guide. With the right methods, you will find that guiding your Aussie is both fun and easy.

Dog training methods have changed little through the years, but they should have. Old-fashioned dog training methods based on force are difficult, ineffective, and no fun for either dog or trainer. Punishment may tell a dog what not to do, but it can't tell a dog what he should do.

Remember that your role should be that of teacher, not drill master; your goal is to teach through guidance, not punishment.

Training Tips

1. Guide, don't force: Aussies already want to please you; your job is to simply show them the way. Forcing them can distract or intimidate them, actually slowing down learning.

2. Train before meals: Your Aussie will work better if his stomach is not full, and will be more responsive to food rewards. Never try to train a sleepy, tired, or hot dog.

3. Happy endings: Begin and end each training session with something the dog can do well. Keep sessions short and fun—no longer than 10 or 15 minutes. Dogs have short attention spans and you will notice that after about 15 minutes their performance will begin to suffer unless a lot of play is involved. To continue to train a tired or bored dog will result in the training of bad habits, resentment in the dog, and frustration for the trainer. Especially when training a young puppy, or when you only have one or two different exercises to practice, quit while you are ahead! Keep your Aussie wanting more, and you will have a happy, willing, obedient partner.

4. Once is enough: Repeating a command over and over, or shouting it louder and louder, never helped anyone, dog or human, understand what is expected of them. Your Aussie is not hard of hearing.

5. The best-laid plans: Finally, nothing will ever go just as perfectly as it seems to in all of the training instructions; however, although there may be setbacks, you *can* train your dog, as long as you remember to be consistent, firm, gentle, realistic, and, most of all, patient.

Timing

The first ingredient in any command is your dog's name. You probably spend a good deal of your day talking, with very few words intended as commands for your dog, so warn your dog that this talk is directed toward him.

Many trainers make the mistake of simultaneously saying the command word *at the same time* that they are placing the dog into position. *This is incorrect.* The command comes immediately before the desired action or position. The crux of training is anticipation; the dog comes

to anticipate that after hearing a command he will be induced to perform some action, and he will eventually perform this action without further assistance from you. On the other hand, when the command and action come at the same time, not only does the dog tend to pay more attention to your action of placing him in position, and less attention to the command

TIP

Higher Education

Teach stationary exercises on a raised surface. This allows you to have eye contact with your dog and gives you a better vantage from which to help your dog learn.

Aussie Advice

A choke collar is not for choking! In fact, it is more correctly termed a slip collar. The proper way to administer a correction with a choke collar is with a *very* gentle snap, then immediate release. The choke collar is placed on the dog so that the ring with the lead attached comes up around the left side of the dog's neck, and through the other ring. If put on backwards, it will not release itself after being tightened (since you will be on the right side of your dog for most training). The choke collar should *never* be left on your Aussie after training sessions; there are too many tragic cases in which a choke collar really did earn its name after being snagged on a fence, bush, or even a playmate's tooth.

word, but the command word loses its predictive value for the dog. Remember: Name, command, action, reward! Don't forget to give your dog a release command such as *"OK!"* to tell him that he is free to go when you're through.

Rewards

Many years ago the idea was perpetuated that dogs should never be trained with food, yet professional animal trainers and animal learning scientists all knew that food training produced excellent results. Only recently has food-motivated training become accepted in training the family dog, and owners are finding dogs that learn faster, mind more reliably, work more eagerly, and have a more trusting dog-owner relationship.

Praise can become a stronger motivator by always praising immediately before a food reward is given. In this way praise becomes a secondary reinforcer. Eventually, the dog can be weaned from the food and will come to work in large part for praise, but food should still be given as reward intermittently.

Food is used initially to guide the dog into position, and then to reward the dog when he is in place. After the dog knows what is expected, the food is held out of sight and only given to the dog when he has performed correctly. Ultimately, the dog is weaned from getting a food reward each time, but still gets one every once in a while. Such a randomized schedule has been shown to be effective in animals and humans.

Professional dog trainers go one step farther. They use a signal (such as that from a clicker) to instantly tell the dog when it has performed correctly. The signal is then followed by a food reward. A clicker signal is used because it is fast, noticeable, and something the dog otherwise does not encounter. In order to apply this technique to the following instructions, whenever giving a treat is mentioned, you should precede it with a clicker signal.

Correct placement of the choke collar.

Training Equipment

Equipment for training should include a 6-foot (1.8-m) and a 20-foot (6-m) lightweight lead. For puppies it is convenient to use one of the lightweight adjustable-size show leads. Most Aussies can be trained with a buckle collar, but a nylon choke collar is also an acceptable choice as long as you know how to use it correctly.

Basic Obedience

It's never too early or too late to start the education of your Aussie. With a very young Aussie, train for even shorter time periods. By the time your Aussie pup (here named "Stinky") reaches six months, he should be familiar with the following commands:

"Watch Me"

A common problem when training any dog is that the dog's attention is elsewhere. You can teach your dog to pay attention to you by teach-

===== T I P =====

Up Against the Wall

If your dog backs up instead of sits down, place his rear against a wall while training the sit.

ing him the *"Watch me"* command. Say *"Stinky, watch me,"* and when he looks in your direction, give him a treat or other reward. Gradually require him to look at you for longer and longer periods before rewarding him. Teach *"Watch me"* before going on to the other commands.

"Sit"

The easiest way to teach the *sit* is to stand in front of your pup and hold a tidbit above his eye level. Say *"Stinky, sit,"* and then move the tidbit toward your pup until it is slightly behind and above his eyes. You may have to keep a hand on his rump to prevent him from jumping up. When the puppy begins to look up and bend his hind legs, praise, then offer the tidbit. Repeat this, requiring the dog to bend his legs more and more until he must be sitting before receiving praise.

"Stay"

Teach your dog to sit and stay until given the release signal before walking through the front door or exiting your car.

Have your dog sit, then say *"Stay"* in a soothing voice (for commands in which the dog is not supposed to move, don't precede the command with the dog's name). If your Aussie attempts to

Training to sit using treats.

get up or lie down, gently but instantly place him back into position. Work up to a few seconds, give a release word ("OK!") and praise and give a tidbit. Next, step out (starting with your right foot) and turn to stand directly in front of your dog while he stays. Work up to longer times, but don't ask a young puppy to stay longer than 30 seconds; the object is not to push your dog to the limit, but to let him succeed. You must increase your times and distances in very small increments. Finally, practice with the dog on lead by the front door or in the car.

"Come"

Coming on command could save your dog's life. You want your puppy to respond to *"Stinky, come"* with the same enthusiasm as though you were setting down his supper; in other words, *"Come"* should always be associated with good things.

Think about what excites your Aussie and makes him run to you. For most young Aussies, the opportunity to chase after you is one of the grandest games ever invented—and of course, most young Aussies will jump at the chance to gobble up a special treat. Combine these two urges and use them to entice your Aussie to come on the run.

The best time to start is when your Aussie is a young puppy, but it is never too late. You will need a helper and an enclosed area; a hallway is perfect for a very young pup. Have your helper gently restrain the puppy while you back away and entice the puppy. Do whatever it takes at first. The point is to get the pup's attention, and to get him struggling to get away and get to you. Only at this point should you call out *"Stinky, come!"* with great enthusiasm, at the same time turning around and

Look Away

Don't stare at your dog during the *stay*, as this is perceived by the dog as a threat and often intimidates him.

running away. Your helper will release the pup at the same time, and you should let him catch up to you. Reward him by playing for a second, then kneel down and give him the special treat. Repeat this several times a day, gradually increasing the distance, taking care never to practice past the time when your pup begins to tire of the game.

Once your puppy has learned the meaning of *"Come,"* move your training outdoors. With the pup on lead, command *"Stinky, come!"* enthusiastically, and quickly run away. When he reaches you, praise and reward. If he ignores you for more than a second, tug on the lead to get the pup's attention, but do not drag him. Response to the *come* command is not one that can be put off until your dog feels like coming. In addition, the longer you separate the tug from the command, the harder it will be for your pup to relate the two and, in the long run, the harder the training will be on the youngster. After the tug, be sure to run back-

wards and make the pup think that it was all part of the grand game.

Next, attach a longer line to the pup, allow him to meander about, and in the midst of his investigations, call, run backwards, and reward. After a few repetitions, drop the long line, let Stinky mosey around a bit, then call. If he begins to come, run away and let him chase you as part of the game. If he doesn't come, pick up the line and give a tug, then run away as usual. If at any time your Aussie runs the other way, never chase him—chase the line, not the dog. The only game an Aussie likes more than chasing you is being chased by you. He will always win. Chase the line, grab it, give it a tug, then run the other way.

As your dog becomes more reliable, you should begin to practice (still on the long line) in the presence of such distractions as other leashed dogs, unfamiliar people, cats or other animals, and cars. In most of these cases you should not let the dog drag the line, but hold on just in case the distractions prove too enticing.

Some dogs develop a habit of dancing around just out of reach of you, considering your futile grabs to be another part of this wonderful game. You can prevent this by requiring your dog to allow you to hold him by the collar before you reward him. Eventually, you may add sitting in front of you as part of the game.

"Down"

When you need your Aussie to stay in one place for a long time, it is best for him to be left in a *down/stay*. Begin teaching the *down* command with the dog in the sitting position. Command *"Stinky, down,"* then show him a tidbit and move it below his nose toward the ground. If he reaches down to get it, give it to

TIP

Come and Get It!

Never have your dog come to you and then scold him for something he has done. In the dog's mind he is being scolded for coming, not for any earlier misdeed. Nor should you call your dog to you at the end of an off-lead walk. You don't want the dog to associate coming to you with relinquishing his freedom. Call him to you several times during the walk, reward him, and praise him, and then send him back out to play.

him. Repeat, requiring him to reach farther down (without lifting his rear from the ground) until he has to lower his elbows to the ground. Never try to force your dog into the *down* position, which can scare a submissive dog and cause a dominant dog to resist. Practice the *down/stay* just as you did the *sit/stay*.

"Heel"

Walking alongside you on lead may be a new experience for a youngster, and many will freeze in their tracks once they discover their freedom is being violated. In this case do not simply drag the pup along, but coax him with food. When the puppy follows you, praise and reward. In this way the pup comes to realize that following you while walking on lead pays off.

Some Aussies have a tendency to forge ahead, pulling their hapless owners behind them. Although at times this may be acceptable to you, at other times it will be annoying and perhaps even dangerous. After all, Aussies are strong! Even if you have no intention of teach-

TIP

Soft Spot

Aussies don't mind learning the *down*, but some mind having to lie on a hard floor. Your initial training will be much easier if you do it on a soft warm surface.

ing a perfect competition *heel*, you need to teach the *heel* as a way of letting your Aussie know it is your turn to be the leader.

Have your Aussie sit in *heel* position; that is, on your left side with its neck next to and parallel with your leg. Say *"Stinky, heel,"* and step off with your left foot first (remember that you stepped off on your right foot when you left your dog on a *stay*; if you are consistent, the foot that moves first will provide an eye-level cue for your dog). During your first few practice sessions you will keep him on a short lead, hold-

━━━━━━ T I P ━━━━━━

Fast Work

When heeling, keep up a pace that requires your Aussie to walk fairly briskly; too slow a pace gives your dog time to sniff, look all around, and in general become distracted; a brisk pace will focus the dog's attention upon you and generally aid training.

Canine Good Citizen Test

In order to formally recognize dogs that behave in public, the AKC offers the Canine Good Citizen (CGC) certificate, which requires your Aussie to

✔ accept a friendly stranger who greets you.

✔ sit politely for petting by a stranger.

✔ allow a stranger to pet and groom him.

✔ walk politely on a loose lead.

✔ walk through a crowd on a lead.

✔ sit and lie down on command and stay in place while on a 20-foot (6-m) line.

✔ calm down after play.

✔ react politely to another dog. React calmly to distractions.

✔ remain calm when held by a stranger for three minutes in the owner's absence. To find a test location, go to *www.akc.org/events/cgc.*

ing him in *heel* position, and of course praising him. The traditional method of letting the dog lunge to the end of the lead and then snapping it back is unfair if you haven't shown the dog what is expected of him at first. Instead, after a few sessions of showing your dog the *heel* position, give him a little more loose lead and use a tidbit to guide him into correct position.

If your Aussie still forges ahead after you have shown him what is expected, pull him back to position with a quick gentle tug, then release, of the lead. If, after a few days practice, your dog still seems oblivious to your efforts, then turn unexpectedly several times; teach your dog that it is his responsibility to keep an eye on you. Keep in mind that every time you do this you cause your Aussie to heel a little bit farther back in relation to you, and

that in the long run, more dogs have a problem with lagging way behind than with forging ahead. In other words, don't go overboard when trying to correct forging. It will tend to self-correct with just a little guidance.

As you progress you will want to add some right, left, and about-faces, and walk at all different speeds. Then practice in different areas (still always on lead) and around different distractions. You can teach your Aussie to sit every time you stop. Vary your routine to combat boredom, and keep training sessions short. Be sure to give the *"OK"* command before allowing your dog to sniff, forge, and meander on lead.

FEEDING YOUR AUSTRALIAN SHEPHERD

Commercial dog foods should meet the Association of American Feed Control Officials' (AAFCO) guidelines for a particular age group of dogs.

Your Aussie's athletic build, as well as his condition, health, and ultimate longevity depend in part upon what food you choose to set in front of him—and all it takes is one dizzying trip through the dog food section of a supermarket, pet supply store, or dog show vendor aisle to leave you utterly baffled. Before you become paralyzed with indecision, keep in mind that dog nutritionists have done most of the work for you, and that as long as your food passes some basic guidelines it will be adequate to sustain your dog's life. It may not make it bloom with condition, however. For that, you do need to do a little investigating on your own.

Food Choices

Almost all commercially available foods have a statement on the container certifying that the food meets AAFCO guidelines. Critics contend that these guidelines are too lenient, and that many pet foods use substandard ingredients. Premium dog foods, available from large pet supply chains, usually use better quality ingredients and exceed AAFCO minimums.

Commercial foods come in dry, canned, and moist varieties. Dry foods are generally healthiest, provide needed chewing action, and are most economical, but they tend to be less appealing. Many people mix them with tastier canned foods which are usually higher in fat and tastier. Semi-moist foods are high in sugar and, although handy for travel, lack the better attributes of the other food types. Dog treats may not always meet AAFCO requirements for a complete diet but are fine as supplements.

Home-prepared diets have become increasingly popular. Such diets have the advantage of being fresh and of using human-quality ingredients. If they are prepared according to recipes devised by certified canine nutritionists, they should have the correct proportion of nutrients. Unlike commercial dog foods, such diets are not customarily tested on generations of dogs, which makes them vulnerable to looking healthy on paper but not being properly digested or utilized. They can also be labor intensive, although large batches can be made and frozen.

Some people prefer to feed their dogs a BARF (Bones And Raw Food) diet, with the idea that such a diet better emulates that of a wild dog. They point out that nobody ever sees wolves eating from a bag of kibble or even cooking their catch of the day. They feed raw meaty bones along with vegetables. Although dogs have better resistance to bacterial food poisoning than do humans, such diets have nonetheless occasionally been associated with food poisoning, often from salmonella, in dogs. Commercially available meats may be awash in contaminated liquids. Perhaps the worst problem with the BARF diets, however, is that most people who claim to use them never bother to find a nutritionally balanced diet but instead rely on friends who advocate a solid diet of chicken wings or some equally unbalanced diet.

What about table scraps? Although too many table scraps can throw off the nutrient balance, a few may actually be healthy. But choose your scraps carefully. Avoid hunks of fat, which can bring on pancreatitis, and avoid the following human foods that are toxic to dogs:

- Onions cause a condition in which the red blood cells are destroyed. Eating an entire onion could be fatal.
- Chocolate contains theobromine, which can cause death in dogs.
- Macadamia nuts cause some dogs to get very ill; the cause isn't understood.
- Raisins and grapes have been associated with kidney failure and extreme sudden toxicity in some dogs.

Nutrition

A balanced diet must have minimal amounts of protein, fat, carbohydrates, vitamins, minerals, and water.

Protein provides the building blocks for bone, muscle, coat, and antibodies. Eggs, followed by meats, have higher quality and more digestible proteins than do plant-derived proteins.

Fat provides energy and aids in the transport of vitamins. Plus it adds taste. Too little fat in the diet (less than 5 percent dry matter) results in dry coats and scaly skin. Too much fat can cause diarrhea, obesity, and a reduced appetite for more nutritious foods.

Carbohydrates abound in plant and grain ingredients. Dogs were the inventors of the low-carb diet, but people have been bulking up their food with low-cost carbohydrates for years. Dogs can't utilize their nutrients from carbohydrates unless the carbs are cooked; even then, they utilize them to different degrees

"He Ate What?"

Dogs can eat a variety of strange things. Some dogs have abnormal desires to ingest nonedible substances, including wood, fabric, or soil. Talk to your veterinarian about possible health problems that could contribute to these specific hungers, and about possible problems that could result from eating these items. The most common and seemingly appalling non-food item eaten by dogs is their own feces. This habit, called coprophagia, has been blamed on boredom, stress, hunger, poor nutrition, and excessively rich nutrition, but none of these has proved a completely satisfactory explanation. Food additives are available that make the stool less savory, and you can also try adding hot pepper to it, but a determined dog will not be deterred and the best cure is immediate removal of all feces. Many puppies experiment with stool-eating but grow out of it.

depending on their source. Carbohydrates from rice are best utilized, followed by potato and corn, and then wheat, oat, and beans. Excessive carbohydrates in the diet can cause diarrhea, flatulence, and poor athletic performance.

Vitamins are essential for normal life functions. Dogs require the following vitamins in their diet: A, D, E, B_1, B_2, B_{12}, niacin, pyridoxine, pantothenic acid, folic acid, and choline. Most dog foods have these vitamins added in their optimal percentages so that supplementing with vitamin tablets is rarely necessary.

Minerals help build tissues and organs and are part of many body fluids and enzymes. Deficiencies or excesses can cause anemia, poor growth, strange appetite, fractures, convulsions, vomiting, weakness, heart problems, and many other disorders. Again, most commercial dog foods have minerals added in their ideal percentages. It is not a good idea to supplement your dog's diet with minerals, especially calcium.

Fiber, such as beet pulp or rice bran, should make up a small part of the dog's diet. It's often used in weight-loss diets to give the dog a full feeling, although its effectiveness is controversial. Too much fiber causes large stool volume and can impair the digestion of other nutrients.

Water is essential for life. It dissolves and transports other nutrients, helps regulate body temperature, and helps lubricate joints. Dehydration can cause or complicate many health problems. Keep a bowl of clean, cool water available for your Aussie at all times.

How much of each nutrient should your dog get? It depends. Growing dogs need more protein, active dogs need more protein and fat, fat dogs need more protein and less fat, and sick dogs need reduction or addition of various ingredients according to their illnesses.

Guaranteed Analysis

The guaranteed analysis represents the worst-case scenario of the minimal percentages of crude protein and crude fat, and maximal percentages of crude fiber and moisture. "Crude" means that the level is determined indirectly, in the case of protein by measuring nitrogen. The drawback is that it doesn't measure protein quality or digestibility.

The fat percentage is handy in comparing the calories a food may contain, since fat has roughly double the calories of protein or carbohydrates. If fiber and moisture content are the same, a higher fat content food will have more calories.

Crude fiber is an estimate of how much of the food is indigestible. Higher levels are often found in weight-reducing diets.

You'll notice that dry foods seem jam packed with nutrition compared to wet foods. That's because wet foods have so much water in them it makes their nutritive content look, well, watered down. To compare dry foods to wet foods, you have to factor out the differing moisture content so you compare them on their dry matter. Here's how: (1) Subtract the listed moisture content from each. (2) Take the remaining number you get (the food's dry matter) and divide it into each listed nutrient percentage. So for a canned food with a listed moisture content of 80 percent and protein of 5 percent, you divide 5 by 20 equals 25. The canned food contains 25 percent protein on a dry matter basis.

Avoiding Fat

The dog's wild ancestor, the wolf, evolved to survive feast and famine, gorging following a kill, but then perhaps waiting several days before another feast. In today's world, dogs can feast daily, and without the period of famine they can easily become obese.

An Aussie in proper weight should have an hourglass figure whether viewed from above or the side. There should be no roll of fat over the withers or rump. The stomach should be slightly tucked up. The ribs should be easily felt through a layer of muscle. The Aussie is an athlete, and should have an athlete's body: lean and muscular.

Overweight Aussies should be fed a high-fiber, low-fat, and medium-protein diet dog food. Such commercially available diet foods, which supply about 15 percent fewer calories per pound, are preferable to the alternative of just feeding less of a fattening food.

Many people find that one of the many pleasures of dog ownership is sharing a special treat with their pet. Rather than giving up this bonding activity, substitute a low-calorie alternative such as rice cakes or carrots. Make sure family members aren't sneaking the dog forbidden tidbits. Keep the dog out of the kitchen or dining area at food preparation or meal times. Schedule a walk immediately following your dinner to get your dog's mind off your leftovers—it will be good for both of you.

If your dog remains overweight, seek your veterinarian's opinion. Heart disease and some endocrine disorders, such as hypothyroidism or Cushing's disease, or the early stages of diabetes, can cause the appearance of obesity and should be ruled out or treated. However, as in humans, most cases of obesity are simply from eating more calories than are expended. Obesity predisposes dogs to joint injuries and heart problems. An obese Aussie cannot enjoy one of its greatest pleasures in life—the ability to run, jump, and frisk with boundless energy.

Changing Diets

If you change from one food to another, do it gradually over several days. One of life's great mysteries is why dogs, who can seemingly scarf down garbage-can bounty without ill effects, can get upset stomachs simply by switching from one dog food to another.

Underweight Aussies may gain weight with puppy food; add water, milk, bouillon, or canned food and heat slightly to increase aroma and palatability. Milk will cause many dogs to have diarrhea, so try only a little bit at first. Try a couple of dog food brands, but if your Aussie still won't eat, you may have to employ some tough love. Many picky eaters are created when their owners begin to spice up their food with especially tasty treats. The dog then refuses to eat unless the preferred treat is offered, and finally learns that if he refuses even that proffered treat, another even tastier enticement will be offered. Give your dog a good, tasty meal, but don't succumb to Aussie blackmail or you may be a slave to your dog's gastronomical whims for years to come.

Your veterinarian should examine your dog if his appetite fails to pick up, or if he can't gain weight. More worrisome would be a dog that suddenly loses his appetite or weight, a possible warning sign of a physical disorder.

A sick or recuperating dog may have to be coaxed into eating. Cat food or meat baby food are both relished by dogs and may entice a dog without an appetite to eat.

Feeding Schedules

Very young puppies should be fed three or four times a day, on a regular schedule. Feed them as much as they care to eat in about 15 minutes. From the age of three to six months, pups should be fed three times daily, and after that, twice daily. Adult dogs can be fed once a day, but it is actually preferable to feed smaller meals twice a day.

If you choose to let the dog "self-feed," leaving food available at all times, monitor his

Food Allergies

Aussies that are allergic to food ingredients are typically allergic to particular proteins. Beef and corn are common culprits. By feeding a bland diet of proteins the dog has never eaten, such as venison, duck, or rabbit, the allergic symptoms (which range from diarrhea to itchiness) should subside. If they do, ingredients are added back one by one until an ingredient is found that triggers the response. You may have to keep your dog on a diet of novel proteins forever—at least until he develops an allergy to it and you must move to another novel protein. Some hypoallergenic diets consist not of novel proteins, but of protein molecules that are too small to cause allergic reactions.

weight to be sure he is not overindulging. Leave only dry food down; canned food spoils rapidly and becomes both unsavory and unhealthy. If your dog overindulges, you will have to intervene.

Water

Water is essential for your Aussie's health and comfort. Don't just keep your dog's water bowl full by topping it up every day. Such a habit allows algae to form along the sides of the bowl, and gives bacteria a chance to multiply. Empty, scrub, and refill the water bowl daily. If the water bowl runs dry, your Aussie may turn to the toilet bowl as an alternative source; in fact, you should make it a practice to keep the lid down, because many dogs view the toilet bowl as an especially deluxe watering hole! It should go without saying that drinking from the toilet is not a healthy practice.

PREVENTIVE HEALTH CA

Choose your veterinarian carefully, and take your duties seriously.

An ounce of prevention really is worth a pound of cure. Preventive medicine encompasses accident prevention, vaccinations, and parasite control, as well as good hygiene and grooming. It is a team effort directed by your veterinarian but undertaken by you.

An Ounce of Prevention

Don't wait until your Aussie is sick to choose a veterinarian. Consider availability, emergency arrangements, facilities, costs, ability to communicate, and experience with Australian Shepherds. Most general veterinarians can provide a wide range of services, but if your dog has a problem that eludes diagnosis or requires specialized treatment, let your veterinarian know if you are willing to be referred to a specialist in that field.

Vaccinations

Without well-timed vaccinations your Aussie can be vulnerable to deadly communicable diseases. Your pup received his early immunity through his dam's colostrum during the first few days of nursing. As long as your pup still has that immunity, any vaccinations you give him won't provide sufficient immunity. But after several weeks that immunity begins to decrease. As his immunity falls, both the chance of a vaccination being effective and the chance of getting a communicable disease rise. The problem is that immunity diminishes at different times in different dogs. So starting at around six weeks of age, a series of vaccinations are given in order to catch the time when they will be effective while leaving as little unprotected time as possible. During this time of uncertainty, it's best not to take your pup around places where unvaccinated dogs may congregate. Some deadly viruses, such as parvovirus, can remain in the soil for six months after an infected dog has shed virus in its feces there.

This doesn't mean you must load up on every vaccine available. Vaccinations are divided into core vaccines, which are advisable for all dogs, and noncore vaccines, which are advisable only for some dogs. Core vaccines are those for rabies, distemper, parvovirus, and hepatitis (using the CAV-2 vaccine, not the CAV-1, which can cause adverse reactions and is still sold by some feed stores). Noncore vaccines include those for leptospirosis, corona virus, tracheobronchitis, Lyme disease, and giardia. Your veterinarian can advise you if your dog's

MDR1 Gene

...er breeds,
...to several
...m. Ivermectin is one
...n drugs used in heart-
...ion. In the prescribed doses for
...on, it is harmless to Aussies. However,
...the larger doses needed for worming or to combat mites, the drug causes neurological symptoms and even death in some, but not all, Aussies. Researchers have traced the problem to a particular gene, called MDR1 (Multi-Drug Resistance 1).

About 32 percent of Aussies, and 49 percent of Miniature Aussies, have at least one copy of the MDR1 gene. Dogs with two copies of the gene are adversely affected, and even dogs with one copy may have some lesser problems.

It's not only ivermectin that causes problems in MDR1 dogs. Other drugs that cause problems in these dogs are selamectin, milbemycin, and moxidectin (antiparasitic agents); loperamide (antidiarrheal agent found in Immodium); acepromazine (tranquilizer and pre-anesthetic agent); butorphanol (analgesic and pre-anesthetic agent); and vincristine, vinblastine, and doxorubicin (chemotherapy agents). Because several of these drugs are commonly used when your dog has surgery, it's a good idea to find out now if your Aussie has the MDR1 gene or genes. Washington State University (*http://www.vetmed.wsu.edu/ announcements/ivermectin/*) offers the test in North America; for other laboratories throughout the world, go to *http://www. ashgi.org/articles/mdr1.htm.*

lifestyle and environment put him at risk for these diseases. Remember, more is not better!

A sample core vaccination protocol for puppies suggests giving a three-injection series at least two weeks apart, with each injection containing distemper (or measles for the first injection), parvovirus, adenovirus 2 (CAV-2), and parainfluenza (CPIV). The series should not end before 12 weeks of age. A booster is given one year later, and then boosters are given every three years. Rabies should be given at 16 weeks of age, with boosters at one to three year intervals according to local law.

The topic of how frequent boosters should be given is currently under scrutiny. Some owners elect to test their dogs' blood titers to various diseases to see if a booster is needed. A high titer generally indicates

protection, but a low titer doesn't mean the dog isn't protected.

Some proponents of natural rearing condemn vaccinations and refuse to use them. They use homeopathic nosodes instead, and point to the fact that their dogs don't get sick as proof that they work. However, their good fortune is probably the result of herd immunity; that is, as long as most other dogs are vaccinated they probably never come in contact with the infectious agents. And no controlled study has ever supported the effectiveness of nosodes. Vaccinations are not without a downside, but they are essential components of your dog's healthy future. Don't take chances.

De-worming

Your pup should have been checked and

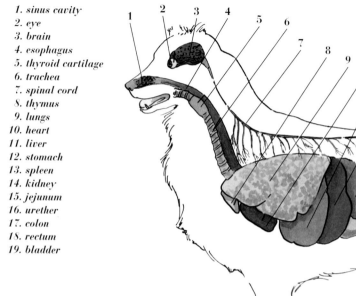

1. sinus cavity
2. eye
3. brain
4. esophagus
5. thyroid cartilage
6. trachea
7. spinal cord
8. thymus
9. lungs
10. heart
11. liver
12. stomach
13. spleen
14. kidney
15. jejunum
16. urether
17. colon
18. rectum
19. bladder

de-wormed if necessary before coming home with you. Most pups have worms at some point because some types of worms lie dormant and protected in the dam until hormonal changes caused by her pregnancy activate them and enable them to infect her puppies. Your pup can also pick up worms from the ground in places where dogs congregate. The best prevention at home is to clean up feces immediately. Some heartworm preventives also prevent many types of worms. Get your pup regular fecal checks for worms, but don't de-worm your pup unnecessarily. Avoid over-the-counter worm medications, which are neither as safe nor effective as those available from your veterinarian.

If you see small, flat, white segments in your dog's stool, he may have tapeworms. Tapeworms are acquired when your pup eats a flea, so the best prevention is flea prevention. Tapeworms require special medication to get rid of them.

Heartworm Prevention

Heartworms can kill your dog. They are carried by mosquitoes, so if there is any chance of a single mosquito biting your Aussie, he needs to be on heartworm preventive medication. Ask your veterinarian when he should begin taking the medication, as it may vary according to your location. Dogs over 6 months of age should be checked for heartworms with a simple blood test before beginning heartworm prevention. The once a month preventive is safe, convenient, and effective. Treatment is available for heartworms, but it's far cheaper, easier, and safer to prevent them.

Spaying and Neutering

Unless you aim to be the kind of breeder you were advised to look for (see page 20), your best plan is to enjoy your Aussie as a companion and leave the breeding to others. Here's why:

An intact (unspayed) female comes into estrus twice a year, usually beginning at around 8 months of age. Each heat period lasts for about three weeks, during which she will have a bloody discharge that will ruin your furnishings or necessitate that she be crated for three weeks or wear little britches (which you will then forget to remove when you let her out to potty, and will then have a real mess on your hands). Her scent, which she will advertise by urinating as much as possible, will advertise your home as a roadside brothel, and you may have lots of uninvited canine suitors camping at your door. If you have an intact male of your own, he will drive you insane

with his relentless panting, whining, shaking, and clawing. It will be the longest three weeks of your life.

If you bred a litter, how would you find homes for the pups? Do you trust that the people who answer your advertisements will give your pup a home as good as yours? Will you commit to being responsible for that pup's well-being for the rest of his life? Will you take all the puppies back if their new owners should tire of them or otherwise not be able to keep them?

Good Aussie breeders make these commitments, and more. They screen for hereditary defects, prove their dogs in some form of competition, educate themselves, and stand by their puppies for a lifetime. They often require that buyers neuter or spay their dogs because they know too well the problems dog breeding can create. They also recognize the health advantages that go along with spaying and neutering.

Intact females are at increased risk of developing breast cancer and pyometra, a potentially fatal infection of the uterus. Spaying negates the possibility of pyometra, and spaying before the first season significantly reduces the chance of breast cancer. Intact males are more likely to develop testicular cancer and prostatitis. The major drawbacks are that each procedure requires surgery and anesthesia, that many spayed and neutered dogs gain weight, and that some spayed females develop urinary incontinence. Talk to your veterinarian and breeder about the pros and cons. In most cases, however, the pros outweigh the cons.

Signs of Illness

Being the link between your dog and his doctor is not an easy job. Since your dog can't talk, you have to interpret his behavioral and physical signs.

Behavior Changes

Sick dogs often lie quietly in a curled position. Irritability, restlessness, hiding, clawing, panting, and trembling may indicate pain. Dogs with abdominal pain often stretch and bow. A dog with breathing difficulties will often refuse to lie down, and if he does, he will keep his head raised. Confusion, head-pressing, or seizures may indicate neurological problems.

- Lethargy is the most common sign of illness. Possible causes include
- Infection (check for fever)
- Anemia (check gum color)
- Circulatory problem (check pulse and gum color)
- Pain (check limbs, neck, back, mouth, eyes, ears, and abdomen for signs)

- Nausea
- Poisoning (check gum color and pupil reaction; look for vomiting or abdominal pain)
- Sudden vision loss
- Cancer
- Metabolic diseases

Intake and Output Changes

Changes in eating, drinking, or elimination patterns often indicate illness.

- Ill dogs often experience loss of appetite, although some endocrine disorders may cause increased appetite.
- Increased thirst, usually with increased urination, may indicate kidney disease or diabetes.
- A sudden and frequent urge to urinate, usually in small amounts, perhaps accompanied by signs of pain, may indicate a urinary tract infection. Painful urination, straining to urinate, or blood in the urine may indicate urinary stones. Inability to urinate is a life-threatening emergency.
- Regurgitating food right after eating can indicate an esophageal problem. Vomiting food after it's been in the stomach can indicate poisoning, blockage, or a host of problems. Consult your veterinarian immediately if your dog vomits feces-like matter (which could indicate an intestinal blockage) or blood (which may resemble coffee grounds) and has accompanying fever or pain, or if the vomiting lasts more than a few hours.
- Diarrhea can result from nervousness, a change in diet or water, food sensitivities, intestinal parasites, infections, poisoning, and many other illnesses. It's not uncommon for dogs to have blood in their diarrhea, but diarrhea with lots of blood, or accompanied by vomiting, fever, or other symptoms of illness

The Five-Minute Checkup

Make several copies of this checklist and keep a record of your dog's home exams.

Date: _____

Weight: _____ Temperature: _____ Pulse: _____

Behavior

Is your dog
- ☐ Restless? ☐ Lethargic? ☐ Weak? ☐ Dizzy?
- ☐ Irritable? ☐ Confused? ☐ Bumping into things?
- ☐ Trembling? ☐ Pacing? ☐ Hiding?
- ☐ Eating more or less than usual? ☐ Drinking more than usual?
- ☐ Urinating more or less than usual, or with straining?
- ☐ Having diarrhea? ☐ Straining to defecate?
- ☐ Just standing with front feet on ground and rear in the air?
- ☐ Vomiting or trying to vomit? ☐ Regurgitating undigested food?
- ☐ Gagging? ☐ Coughing? ☐ Breathing rapidly at rest?
- ☐ Spitting up froth? ☐ Pawing at throat? ☐ Snorting? ☐ Limping?

Physical Exam

Hydration:	☐ Dry sticky gums? ☐ Skin that doesn't pop back when strectched?
Gum color:	☐ Pink (good) ☐ Bright red ☐ Bluish ☐ Whitish ☐ Red spots
Gums:	☐ Swellings? ☐ Bleeding? ☐ Sores? ☐ Growths?
Teeth:	☐ Loose? ☐ Painful? ☐ Dirty? ☐ Bad breath?
Nose:	☐ Thick or colored discharge? ☐ Cracking? ☐ Pinched? ☐ Sores?
Eyes:	☐ Tearing? ☐ Mucous discharge? ☐ Dull surface? ☐ Squinting?
	☐ Swelling? ☐ Redness? ☐ Unequal pupils? ☐ Pawing at eyes?
Ears:	☐ Bad smell? ☐ Redness? ☐ Abundant debris? ☐ Scabby ear tips?
	☐ Head shaking? ☐ Head tilt? ☐ Ear scratching? ☐ Painfulness?
Feet:	☐ Long or split nails? ☐ Cut pads? ☐ Swollen or misaligned toes?
Skin:	☐ Parasites? ☐ Black grains (flea dirt)? ☐ Hair loss? ☐ Scabs?
	☐ Greasy patches? ☐ Bad odor? ☐ Lumps?
Anal and genital regions:	☐ Swelling? ☐ Discharge? ☐ Redness?
	☐ Bloody urine? ☐ Bloody or blackened diarrhea?
	☐ Worms in stool or around anus? ☐ Scooting rear? ☐ Licking rear?
Abdomen:	☐ Bloating? ____
Body:	☐ Asymmetrical bones or muscles? ☐ Lumps? ☐ Weight change?

If you answered "yes" to anything abnormal in the checklist, it's worth a call to your veterinarian. Refer to the text for more information.

warrants a call to the veterinarian. Bright red blood indicates a source lower in the digestive tract, while dark black tarry stools indicate a source higher in the digestive tract.

Coughing

Coughing can be caused by foreign bodies, tracheal collapse, tumors, kennel cough, and heart disease, among others. Any cough lasting longer than a few days or accompanied by weakness or difficulty breathing warrants a veterinary exam.

Congestive heart failure causes coughing and breathing difficulties, mainly after exercise and at night and early morning.

Kennel cough is a communicable airborne disease caused by several infectious agents. It is characterized by a gagging or honking cough, often a week after being around infected dogs.

Physical Changes

Sometimes you need to check over your dog piece by piece.

Mouth: If you think your Aussie is sick, one of the first things to check is his gum color. Gums should be a deep pink, and if you press with your thumb, they should return to pink within 2 seconds after lifting your thumb (a longer time suggests a circulatory problem). Very pale gums may indicate anemia, shock, or poor circulation. Bluish gums or tongue can mean a life-threatening lack of oxygen. Bright red gums may indicate overheating or carbon monoxide poisoning, and yellow gums, jaundice. Tiny red splotches may indicate a blood-clotting problem. Tooth and gum problems will often cause bad breath and pain.

Nose: A nasal discharge may indicate a respiratory illness or other disease, or a foreign body or infection of the nose. A cracked nose pad may just be an overly dry nose that needs to be moisturized, or it could be caused by a disease.

Eyes: Squinting or pawing at the eye can arise from pain. Swelling and redness may indicate glaucoma, a scratched cornea, or several other problems. Profuse tear discharge may be caused by a foreign body, scratched cornea, or blocked tear drainage duct. Thick mucus and a dull-appearing surface may indicate "dry eye" (keratoconjunctivitis sicca, or KCS).

Ears: Inflamed or painful ears can result from infection or parasites. See page 64 for more about ears.

Medications

To give a pill, open your dog's mouth and place the pill well in the rear of the mouth. Close the mouth and gently stroke the throat until he swallows. Or just hide the pill in some cream cheese or liverwurst and watch to make sure he eats it.

To give liquid medication, place the liquid in the side of the mouth and let the dog lap it down. Don't squirt it in so that the dog inhales it.

Always give the full course of medications prescribed by your veterinarian.

Never give human medications unless your veterinarian tells you to. Some human medications work on dogs but must be used at different strengths, and some have no effect or bad effects on dogs.

Feet: Foot problems can account for limping. Cut long or split nails short (see page 74), and protect cut pads. Swollen toes could be from infection or an orthopedic problem.

Skin: Parasites, allergies, and infections can cause many skin problems (see page 63). Lumps on the skin may or may not be serious but warrant a veterinary examination.

Anus: Repeated diarrhea can cause an irritated anal area. Repeated scooting or licking can be from diarrhea, parasites, or especially impacted anal sacs. The anal sacs are two sacs filled with smelly brown liquid that normally is excreted with the feces or in times of fright. In some cases, the material can't get out. This is especially true if the tail twists sharply to one side, which can compress one duct. The sac becomes uncomfortably distended, sometimes becoming infected. It may swell outward, even

appearing to be a tumor, and often finally bursting. Your veterinarian can manually express the contents.

Temperature: To take your dog's temperature, lubricate a rectal thermometer and insert it about 2 inches (5 cm) into the dog's anus, leaving it there for about a minute. Normal is from 101 to 102°F (38.3 to 38.8°C). If the temperature is 103°F (39.4°C) or above, call your veterinarian for advice. This is not usually an emergency.

105°F (40.5°C) or above, go to your veterinarian. This is probably an emergency; 106°F (41.1°C) or above is dangerous. Try to cool your dog.

98°F (36.7°C) or below, call your veterinarian for advice. Try to warm your dog.

96°F (35.6°C) or below, go to your veterinarian. Treat for hypothermia on the way by warming your dog.

Pulse: To check the pulse, cup your hand around the top of your dog's rear leg so your fingers are near the top almost where the leg joins the body. Feel for the pulse in the femoral artery. Normal adult Aussie pulse rate is 70 to 120 beats per minute.

Hydration: Check hydration by touching the gums, which should be slick, not sticky, or by lifting the skin on the back and letting it go. It should snap back into place quickly, not remain tented. Sticky gums and tented skin indicate dehydration. If your dog has been vomiting or has diarrhea, he may instantly lose any water you give him, in which case your veterinarian may need to give your dog fluids under the skin or, better, in a vein.

External Parasites: Ticks and fleas are age-old pests that have only recently been on the losing side.

Fleas: In the past, dog owners sprayed their dogs and yards with poisons until it seemed the people and dogs might die before the fleas did. It was expensive, time consuming, and potentially dangerous. Newer products have a higher initial purchase price but are cheaper in the long run because they work and need only be reapplied every few months. Most of these products are available only from your veterinarian, although some discount products try to sound like they work the same. Look for a product with one of the following ingredients:

- Imidacloprid: a self-distributing liquid that kills fleas within a day and continues for a month. It can withstand water, but not repeated bathing.
- Fipronil: a spray or self-distributing liquid that collects in the hair follicles and wicks out over time. It kills fleas for up to

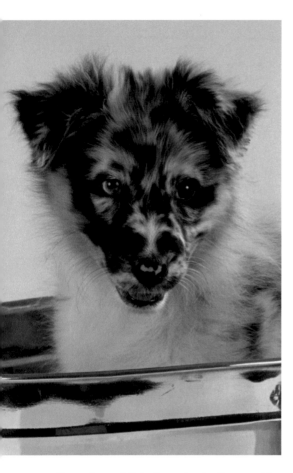

so it's mostly for a quick fix of heavily infested dogs.

- Lufenuron, methoprene, or fenoxycarb: chemicals that interfere with the hatching of flea eggs.

Most over-the-counter products are permethrin based, which isn't resistant to water and doesn't kill fleas for long. Flea populations can easily become resistant to it. In fact, fleas can become resistant to any treatment, so the best strategy is to change products frequently and to include the use of both a flea killer and a flea egg killer. Avoid cholinesterase-inhibiting products; although fairly effective, they have been known to kill dogs when overused or used in conjunction with some wormers or yard insect poisons. And don't bother with the ultrasound, brewer's yeast, or garlic; studies have shown them to be ineffective.

Ticks: Ticks are harder to kill. The same fipronil flea product will kill ticks, but not immediately. Amitraz tick collars are also effective, but they are not perfect. Regardless, if you're in a tick-infested area, you'll need to supplement by feeling your Aussie daily (he'll like the extra petting) and paying close attention around his ears, neck, and between his toes. To remove a tick, use a tissue or tweezers and grasp the tick as close to the skin as possible. Pull slowly, trying not to lose the head or squeeze the contents back into the dog. Even if you get the head with the tick, it will often leave a bump for several days.

Ticks can transmit several diseases. A vaccination is available for Lyme disease, but it's not advisable for dogs that don't live in Lyme endemic areas. Consult your veterinarian as to whether it's advisable in your area. Of greater concern is erhlichiosis, a potentially fatal dis-

3 months and ticks for a shorter time, and is resistant to bathing.

- Selamectin: a self-distributing liquid that kills fleas for one month. It also kills ear mites and several internal parasites and acts as a heartworm preventive. Note: Dogs with the MDR1 gene (see page 54) may be sensitive to selamectin.
- Nytenpyram: oral medication that starts killing fleas in 20 minutes; all fleas are killed in 4 hours. It has almost no residual activity,

ease that cripples the immune system and often has vague symptoms. Other tick-borne diseases include Rocky Mountain spotted fever and babesiosis. Your veterinarian can order blood tests if these conditions are suspected.

Mites: Mites can also cause problems. Sarcoptic mites cause sarcoptic mange, an intensely itchy disorder that you can catch. It's often characterized by small bumps and crusts on the ear tips, abdomen, elbows, and hocks. The condition can be treated with repeated shampoos or with an injection.

Demodex mites cause demodectic mange, a noncontagious but often difficult to treat condition. A couple of small patches in a puppy are commonplace and will usually go away on their own, but many such patches or a generalized condition must be treated with repeated dips or with drug therapy. Cases involving the feet can be especially difficult to cure.

Skin Problems

Flea allergy dermatitis (FAD) is the most common of all skin problems. Itchy, crusted bumps with hair loss in the region around the rump, especially at the base of the tail, results from a flea bite (actually, the flea's saliva) anywhere on the dog's body.

Besides FAD, dogs can have allergic reactions to pollens or other inhaled allergens. Allergies to weeds can manifest themselves between the dog's toes. Suspect them when you see the dog constantly licking his feet, or when the feet are stained pink from saliva. Food allergies can also occur. New blood tests for antibodies are much easier and less expensive (though not as comprehensive) than the traditional intradermal skin testing.

Pyoderma, with pus-filled bumps and crusting, is another common skin disease. *Impetigo* is characterized by such bumps and crusting most often in the groin area of puppies. Both are treated with antibiotics and antibacterial shampoos.

A reddened, moist, itchy spot that suddenly appears is most likely a *"hot spot" (pyotraumatic dermatitis),* which arises from an itch-scratch-chew cycle resulting most commonly from fleas or flea allergy. Wash the area with an oatmeal-based shampoo, and prevent the dog from further chewing. Use an Elizabethan collar (available from your veterinarian or you can fashion one from a plastic pail), or an antichew preparation. Your veterinarian can also prescribe anti-inflammatory medication. As a temporary measure, you can give an allergy pill (Benadryl—ask your veterinarian about dosage), which alleviates some itching and causes drowsiness, both of which should decrease chewing.

In *seborrhea,* there may be excessive dandruff or greasiness, often with excessive earwax and rancid odor. Treatment is with antiseborrheic shampoos or diet change.

Hair may be lost in a bilaterally symmetric pattern, without itching, due to hypothyroidism, Cushing's syndrome, or testicular tumors.

Doggy odor is not only offensive, it is unnatural. Don't exile the dog, or hold your breath. If a bath doesn't produce results, it's time to use your nose to sniff out the source of the problem. Infection is a common cause of bad odor; check the mouth, ears, feet, and genitals. Generalized bad odor can indicate a skin problem, such as seborrhea. Don't ignore bad odor, and don't make your dog take the blame for something you need to fix.

HOW-TO: GROOMING

Brushing

Most Aussies have medium-length hair that should be brushed at least once a week. A slicker brush removes dead hair; in periods of intense shedding you can also use a shedding blade. Use a pin brush if you are trying to save coat. Be sure to brush down to the skin, and don't neglect the areas behind the ears or under the armpits—both prime sites for mats. If you find a mat, spray it with a detangler and try to split it lengthwise and then split it again. Remember to brush the hair out of the mat, not the mat out of the hair.

Bathing

Dog skin has a pH of 7.5, while human skin has a pH of 5.5; therefore, bathing in a shampoo formulated for the pH of human skin can lead to scaling and irritation. You will generally get better results with a shampoo made for dogs. Most shampoos will kill fleas even if not especially formulated as a flea shampoo, but none has any residual killing action on fleas, so, in general, flea shampoos are not a good buy. No dog owner should be without one of the shampoos that requires no water or rinsing; these are wonderful for puppies, spot-baths, and emergencies.

Several therapeutic shampoos are available for various skin problems. Dry scaly skin: moisturizing shampoos; excessive scale and dandruff: antiseborrheic shampoos; damaged skin: antimicrobials; itchy skin: oatmeal-based antipruritics.

Ear Care

The dog's ear canal is made up of an initial long vertical segment that then abruptly angles to run horizontally toward the skull. This configuration provides a moist environment in which various ear infections can flourish, especially in a dog with hanging ears. It is fairly simple to keep the Aussie's ears healthy by checking them regularly and not allowing moisture or debris to build up in them.

Signs of ear problems include inflammation, discharge, debris, foul odor, pain, scratching, shaking, tilting of the head, or circling to one side. Extreme pain may indicate a ruptured eardrum. Ear problems can be difficult to cure once they have become established, so early veterinary attention is crucial. Bacterial and fungal infections, ear mites or ticks, foreign bodies, inhalant allergies, seborrhea, or hypothyroidism are possible underlying problems. Grass awns are one of the most com-

mon causes of ear problems in dogs that spend time outdoors. Keep the ear lubricated with mineral oil, and seek veterinary treatment as soon as possible.

Ear mites, which are often found in puppies, are highly contagious and intensely irritating. Affected dogs will shake their head, scratch their ears, and carry their head sideways. The ear mite's signature is a dark, dry, waxy buildup resembling coffee grounds in the ear canal, usually of both ears. This material is actually dried blood mixed with earwax. Over-the-counter ear mite preparations can cause worse irritation; therefore, ear mites are best treated by your veterinarian.

Apply ear mite drops daily for at least a week, and possibly a month. Because these mites are also found in the dog's fur, you should also bathe the pet weekly with a pyrethrin-based shampoo, or apply a pyrethrin flea dip, powder, or spray.

Nail Care

You must trim your dog's nails every week or two to prevent discomfort or even lameness.

Begin by cutting the very tips of your puppy's nails every week, taking special care not to cut the "quick" (the central core of blood vessels

The ear canal.

It is important to brush your Aussie's teeth to prevent infection from plaque and tartar. Left: an infected tooth. Right: a healthy tooth.

and nerve endings). You may find it easiest to cut the nails by holding the foot backwards, much as a horse's hoof is held when being shod. This way your Aussie can't see what's going on, and you can see the bottom of the nail. Here you will see a solid core culminating in a hollowed nail. Cut the tip up to the core, but not beyond. On occasion you will slip up and cause the nail to bleed, which is best stopped by styptic powder; if this is not available, dip the nail in flour or hold a wet tea bag to it.

Dental Care

Tooth plaque and tartar contribute to bad breath and health problems. Dry food, hard dog biscuits, and nylabone chewies are helpful, but not totally effective, at removing plaque. Brushing your Aussie's teeth once or twice weekly (optimally daily) with a child's toothbrush and *doggy toothpaste* is the best plaque remover. If not removed, plaque will attract bacteria and minerals, which will harden into tartar. If you cannot brush, your veterinarian can supply a cleansing solution that will help

to kill plaque-forming bacteria. You may have to have your veterinarian clean your dog's teeth as often as once a year.

Neglected plaque and tartar can cause infections to form along the gum line. The infection can gradually work its way down the sides of the tooth until the entire root is undermined. The tissues and bone around the tooth erode, and the tooth finally falls out. Meanwhile, the bacteria may have entered the bloodstream and traveled throughout the body, causing infection in the kidneys and heart valves. Neglecting your dog's teeth could kill your dog.

Between four and seven months of age, Aussie puppies will begin to shed their baby teeth. Often, deciduous (baby) teeth, especially the canines (fangs), are not shed, so that the permanent tooth grows in beside the baby tooth. If this condition persists for over a week, consult your veterinarian. Retained baby teeth can cause misalignment of adult teeth. Correct occlusion is important for good dental health. In a correct Aussie bite, the top incisors should fit snugly in front of the bottom incisors.

HEALTH PROBLEMS

You and your veterinarian will form a team that will work together to protect your Aussie's health.

Your home care maintenance can go only so far in ensuring your Aussie's healthy status. No matter how diligent you are, eventually your Aussie will need professional medical attention. A good veterinarian will also be needed to monitor your dog's internal signs by way of blood tests and other procedures.

Blood Work

Your Aussie's blood can provide valuable clues about his state of health, which is why your veterinarian will often want a blood sample if your dog is ill. In fact, it is a good idea to have blood values for your Aussie when he is well as a source of later comparison if he ever becomes ill. Also, you should insist on such blood tests before your dog undergoes surgery to ensure that he is healthy enough for the procedure. The most common tests are the complete blood count (CBC) and the blood chemistry test ("Chem panel"). Many other specialized tests are fairly common.

Emergency Situations

Even experienced dog owners have a diffi-cult time deciding what constitutes a true emergency; when in doubt, err on the side of caution and call the emergency clinic or your veterinarian for an opinion.

Be Prepared

Because there are no paramedics for dogs, you must assume the role of paramedic and ambu-lance driver in case of an emergency. Now is the time to prepare for these life-saving roles. Know the phone number and location of the emergency veterinarian in your area. Keep the number next to the phone; don't rely on your memory during an emergency situation. Study the emergency procedures described in this chapter, and keep this guide handy. Misplaced instructions can result in the loss of critical time. Always keep enough fuel in your car to make it to the emergency clinic without stopping for gas. Finally, stay calm. It will help you help your dog, and will help your dog stay calm as well. A calm dog is less likely to go into shock.

For the following situations, administer first aid and seek veterinary attention.

Poisoning

Symptoms and treatment vary depending upon the specific poison. In most cases, home treatment is not advisable. If in doubt about

Steps to Take in an Emergency
✔ Make sure you and the dog are in a safe location.
✔ Make sure breathing passages are open. Remove any collar and check the mouth and throat.
✔ Move the dog as little and as gently as possible.
✔ Control any bleeding.
✔ Check breathing, pulse, and consciousness.
✔ Check for signs of shock (very pale gums, weakness, unresponsiveness, faint pulse, shivering). Treat by keeping the dog warm and calm.
✔ Never use force or do anything that causes extreme discomfort.
✔ Never remove an impaled object (unless it is blocking the airway).

whether poison was ingested, call the veterinarian anyway. If possible, bring the poison and its container with you to the veterinarian.

Two of the most common and life-threatening poisons eaten by dogs are Warfarin (rodent poison) and, especially, ethylene glycol (antifreeze). Veterinary treatment must be obtained within two to four hours of ingestion of even tiny amounts of these substances if the dog's life is to be saved. *Do not wait for symptoms.* By the time symptoms of antifreeze poisoning are evident, it is usually too late to save the dog.

Signs of poisoning vary according to the type of poison, but commonly include vomiting, convulsions, staggering, and collapse.

Call the veterinary poison control hotline (1-900-680-0000 or 1-800-548-2423; note that calls will incur a $20 to $30 charge) and give as much information as possible. Induce vomiting (except in the cases outlined below) by giving either hydrogen peroxide (mixed 1:1 with water), saltwater, or dry mustard and water. Get the dog to the veterinarian at once.

Do not induce vomiting if the poison was an acid, alkali, petroleum product, solvent, cleaner, tranquilizer, or if a sharp object was swallowed; also do not induce vomiting if the dog is severely depressed, convulsing, comatose, or if over two hours have passed since ingestion. If the dog is not convulsing or unconscious: dilute the poison by giving milk, vegetable oil, or egg whites. Activated charcoal can adsorb many toxins. Baking soda or milk of magnesia can be given for ingested acids, and vinegar or lemon juice for ingested alkalis.

Seizures
A dog undergoing a seizure may drool, become stiff, or have uncontrollable muscle spasms.

Wrap the dog securely in a blanket to prevent him from injuring himself on furniture or stairs. Remove other dogs from the area (they may attack the convulsing dog). Never put your hands—or anything—in a convulsing dog's mouth. Treat for shock. Make note of all characteristics and sequences of seizure activity, which can help to diagnose the cause.

Bleeding
Consider wounds to be an emergency if there is profuse bleeding, if they are extremely deep, or if they open to the chest cavity, abdominal cavity, or head.

Control massive bleeding first. Cover the wound with a clean dressing and apply pressure; apply more dressings over the others until the bleeding stops. Also elevate the wound site, and apply a cold pack to the site. If an extremity is involved, apply pressure to the closest pressure point as follows:

✔ For a front leg: inside of the front leg just above the elbow.

✔ For a rear leg: inside of the thigh where the femoral artery crosses the thighbone.

Use a tourniquet only in life-threatening situations and when all other attempts have failed. Check for signs of shock.

Sucking chest wounds: Place a sheet of plastic or other nonporous material over the hole and bandage it to make as airtight a seal as possible.

Abdominal wounds: Place a warm, wet, sterile dressing over any protruding internal organs; cover with a bandage or towel. Do not attempt to push organs back into the dog.

Pressure points.

Head wounds: Apply gentle pressure to control bleeding. Monitor for loss of consciousness or shock and treat accordingly.

Heatstroke

Rapid, loud breathing, abundant thick saliva, bright red mucous membranes, and a high rectal temperature are earlier signs of heatstroke. Later signs include unsteadiness, diarrhea, and coma.

The Medicine Chest
✔ rectal thermometer
✔ scissors
✔ tweezers
✔ sterile gauze dressings
✔ self-adhesive bandage (such as Vet-Wrap)
✔ instant cold compress
✔ antidiarrhea medication
✔ ophthalmic ointment
✔ soap
✔ antiseptic skin ointment
✔ hydrogen peroxide
✔ clean sponge
✔ pen light
✔ syringe
✔ towel
✔ stethoscope (optional)
✔ oxygen (optional)
✔ first aid instructions
✔ veterinarian and emergency clinic numbers
✔ poison control center number

Wet the dog down and place it in front of a fan. If this is not possible, immerse the dog in cool water. *Do not plunge the dog in ice water;* the resulting constriction of peripheral blood vessels can make the situation worse. Offer small amounts of water for drinking. You must lower your dog's body temperature quickly, but do not lower it below 100°F (37.8°C). Stop cooling the dog when his temperature reaches 103°F (39.4°C).

Hypothermia

Shivering, cold-feeling, and sluggishness are signs of a dog that has become excessively chilled. Later signs include a very low—under 95°F (35°C)—body temperature, slow pulse and breathing rates, and coma.

Warm the dog gradually. Wrap him in a blanket (preferably one that has been warmed in the dryer). Place plastic bottles filled with hot water outside the blankets (not touching the dog). You can also place a plastic tarp over the blanket, making sure the dog's head is not covered. Monitor the temperature. Stop warming when the temperature reaches 101°F (38.3°C).

Sickness

If a problem persists for more than a couple of days, it is worth getting your veterinarian's opinion. Following is an outline of the most common symptoms and some of their possible causes.

Vomiting

Vomiting is a common occurrence that may or may not indicate a serious problem. Vomiting after eating grass is not unusual and usually of no great concern. Overeating is a common cause of occasional vomiting in puppies, especially if they follow eating with playing. Feed smaller meals more frequently if this becomes a problem. Vomiting immediately after meals could indicate an obstruction of the esophagus. Repeated vomiting could indicate that the dog has eaten spoiled food, undigestible objects, or may have a gastrointestinal problem. Veterinary advice should be sought. Meanwhile, withhold food (or feed as directed for diarrhea), and restrict water.

Consult your veterinarian immediately if your dog vomits a foul substance resembling fecal matter (indicating a blockage in the intestinal tract), blood (partially digested blood resembling coffee grounds), or if there is projectile or continued vomiting. Sporadic vomiting with poor appetite and generally poor condition could indicate internal parasites or a more serious internal disease.

Diarrhea

Diarrhea can result from overexcitement or nervousness, a change in diet or water, sensitivity to certain foods, overeating, intestinal parasites, viral or bacterial infections, or ingestion of toxic substances. Bloody diarrhea, diarrhea with vomiting, fever, or other signs of toxicity, or a diarrhea that lasts for more than a day should not be allowed to continue without veterinary advice. Some of these could be symptomatic of potentially fatal disorders.

Less severe diarrhea can be treated at home by withholding or severely restricting food and water for 24 hours. Ice cubes can be given to satisfy thirst. Administer human diarrhea medication in the same weight dosage as recommended for humans. A bland diet consisting of rice, tapioca, or cooked macaroni, along with cottage cheese or tofu for protein, should be given for several days. Feed nothing else. The intestinal tract needs time off in order to heal.

Coughing

Allergies, foreign bodies, pneumonia, parasites, tracheal collapse, tumors, and especially kennel cough and heart disease can all cause coughing.

Kennel cough is a highly communicable airborne disease caused by several different infectious agents. It is characterized by a gagging cough arising about a week after exposure. Inoculations are available and are an especially good idea if you plan to have your dog around other dogs at training classes or while being boarded.

Heart disease can result in coughing, most often following exercise or in the evening. Affected dogs will often lie down and point their nose in the air in order to breathe better.

Any persistent cough should be checked by your veterinarian.

Urinary Tract Diseases

If your dog has difficulty or pain in urination, urinates suddenly and often but in small amounts, or passes cloudy or bloody urine, it may be suffering from an ailment of the bladder, urethra, or prostate. Dribbling of urine during sleep can indicate a hormonal problem. Urinalysis and a rectal exam by your veterinarian are necessary to diagnose the exact nature of the problem. Bladder infections must be treated promptly to prevent the infection from reaching the kidneys.

Blockage of urine can result in death. Inability to urinate requires immediate emergency veterinary attention.

Kidney disease, ultimately leading to kidney failure, is one of the most common ailments of older dogs. The earliest symptom is usually increased urination. Although the excessive urination may cause problems in keeping your house clean or your night's sleep intact, never try to restrict water from a dog with kidney disease.

Increased urination can also be a sign of diabetes or a urinary tract infection. Your veterinarian can discover the cause with some simple tests, and each of these conditions can be treated.

In males, infections of the *prostate gland* can lead to repeated urinary tract infections, and sometimes painful defecation or blood and pus in the urine. Castration and long-term antibiotic therapy is required for improvement.

Impacted Anal Sacs

Constant licking of the anus or scooting of the anus along the ground are characteristic signs of anal sac impaction. Dogs have two anal sacs that are normally emptied by rectal pressure during defecation. Their musky-smelling contents may also be forcibly ejected when a dog is extremely frightened. Sometimes they fail to empty properly and become impacted or infected. This is more common in obese dogs, dogs with allergies or seborrhea, and dogs that seldom have firm stools. Impacted sacs cause extreme discomfort and can become infected. Treatment consists of manually emptying the sacs and administering antibiotics. As a last resort, the sacs may be removed surgically.

Nasal Solar Dermatitis ("Collie Nose")

This condition is now considered to be a type of autoimmune condition called discoid lupus erythematosus (DLE), in which the body's own immune system turns against the cells of the outer nose. The nose loses its dark pigmentation, becomes reddened, scaly, crusted, and, eventually, ulcerated. Exposure to the sun worsens the condition. Although the hereditary nature is not understood, because it is more common in certain breeds (including Aussies and most collie types) it is assumed to have a genetic component. As in most autoimmune diseases, females are more often affected than males. Treatment is with a combination of sunscreens, anti-inflammatory drugs, and, in severe cases, drugs to suppress the immune system. Although it is reported in Aussies, it is nonetheless uncommon.

Endocrine Disorders

The most widespread hormone-related disorders in the dog are diabetes, hypothyroidism, and Cushing's syndrome. The most common of these, *hypothyroidism,* also has the least obvious symptoms, which may include weight gain, lethargy, and coat problems such as oiliness, dullness, *symmetrical* hair loss, and hair that is easily pulled out.

The hallmark of *diabetes* is increased drinking and urination, and sometimes increased appetite with weight loss.

Cushing's syndrome (hyperadrenocorticism) is seen mostly in older dogs, and is characterized by increased drinking and urination, pot-bellied appearance, symmetrical hair loss on the body, darkened skin, and susceptibility to infections.

All of these conditions can be diagnosed with simple tests, and can be treated with drugs by your veterinarian.

Eye Problems

Aussies generally have healthy eyes, but are subject to several hereditary eye disorders (see page 15). An exam by a veterinary ophthalmologist is essential for any Aussie contemplated as breeding stock.

Squinting or tearing can be due to an irritated cornea or foreign body. Examine under the lids and flood the eye with saline solution, or use a moist cotton swab to remove any debris. If no improvement is seen after a day, have your veterinarian take a look. A watery discharge without squinting can be a symptom of allergies or a tear drainage problem. A clogged tear drainage duct can cause the tears to drain onto the face rather than the normal drainage through the nose. Your veterinarian can diagnose a drainage problem with a simple test.

For contact with eye irritants, flush the eye for five minutes with water or saline solution. For injuries, cover with clean gauze soaked in water or saline solution.

As your Aussie ages, it is natural that the lens of the eye becomes a little hazy; you will notice this as a slightly grayish appearance behind the pupils. If this occurs at a young age, or if the lens looks white or opaque, ask your veterinarian to check your dog for *cataracts.* In cataracts the lens becomes so opaque that light can no longer reach the retina; as in humans, the lens can be surgically replaced with an artificial lens.

Any time your dog's pupils do not react to light or when one eye reacts differently from another, take it to the veterinarian immediately. It could indicate a serious ocular or neurological problem. The eyes are such complex and sensitive organs; you should always be cautious and seek veterinary help.

Cancer

Cancer is one of the most common killers in all dogs, and Aussies are no exception. A recent survey pinpointed two types of cancer as striking Aussies far more frequently that others: hemangiosarcoma and lymphoma. They tend to strike middle-age and older dogs, with a median age of just over nine years.

Hemangiosarcoma is a cancer of the blood vessel lining and is found most often in the spleen, heart, liver, lungs, and skin. Most often, the dog seems perfectly healthy until he collapses with signs of shock, including very pale gums. The problem is that the tumor is bleeding internally. The dog may recover temporarily, or may die from internal bleeding. Sadly, there is no effective treatment except for the skin form of hemagiosarcoma.

Lymphoma is cancer of the lymph system. It's most often discovered when the owner notices the lymph nodes are greatly enlarged. Depending on how many lymph nodes are involved, chemotherapy may be effective.

Dogs respond well to chemotherapy, so if your Aussie is diagnosed with a cancer that is responsive to chemo, don't dismiss the idea because you think it will make your dog too sick. As with all chemotherapy, the sooner it's started, the better.

Lameness

Limping may or may not indicate a serious problem. *Mild* lameness should be treated by complete rest; if it still persists after three days your dog will need to be examined by his veterinarian. Ice packs may help minimize swelling if applied immediately after an injury. Aspirin or other prescription medications may alleviate some of the discomfort of injuries, but never give them if your dog is on its way to surgery. If you administer pain medication, you must confine your dog; lack of pain could encourage it to use the injured limb, ultimately resulting in further injury.

Fractures

Any time a dog is lame and also exhibits swelling or deformation of the affected leg, extreme pain, or grinding or popping sounds, it could indicate a break or another serious problem. It is imperative that the fractured area not be further traumatized by attempts to immobilize it; if in doubt, leave it alone and seek veterinary attention.

Feet and Toes

- Examine the feet of a lame dog for burrs, cuts, peeled pads, or misaligned toes. Split or broken nails can be treated by cutting the nail as short as possible and soaking it in warm salt water. Apply an antibiotic and then a human fingernail mender, followed by a bandage.
- Cuts and peeled pads should be carefully flushed with warm water, and an antibacterial ointment applied. Cover the area with gauze, then wrap the foot with Vet-Wrap (a stretchable bandage that clings to itself). You can also add padding. Change the dressing twice daily (or any time it gets wet) and restrict exercise until it heals. If you need a quick fix for a minor injury, you can fashion a makeshift pad by adhering a thin piece of rubber or leather to the bottom of the pad with Super-Glue, or you can apply a coat of Nu-Skin (available at drugstores) if the injury is not too extensive. Peeled pads are very painful. A local anesthetic such as non-steroidal hemorrhoid cream or a topical

toothache salve can help ease some of the discomfort. Deep cuts or extensive peeling should be checked by your veterinarian.

Knee Injuries

Knee injuries, especially of the cruciate ligaments, are common in dogs, especially overweight dogs. They can also arise when the dog is pushed sideways while running. Most cruciate tears do not mend on their own; still, cruciate surgery requires a commitment to careful nursing and should not be undertaken casually.

Puppy Problems

Puppies are especially susceptible to bone and joint injuries, and should never be allowed to jump from high places or run until exhausted. Persistent limping in puppies may result from one of several developmental bone problems, and should be checked by the veterinarian. Both puppies and adults should be discouraged from romping on slippery floors that could cause them to lose their footing.

Older Dogs

In older dogs, or dogs with a previous injury, limping is often the result of osteoarthritis. Arthritis can be treated with aspirin, but should be done so only under veterinary supervision. Do not use naxopren. Your veterinarian can prescribe drugs that may help greatly. Any time a young or middle-aged dog shows signs of arthritis, especially in a joint that has not been previously injured, he should be examined by his veterinarian.

HOW-TO: FIRST AID

In an emergency, first check to see if the dog is responsive by calling its name or tapping on its head. If it is not, quickly assess the ABCs of first aid:

A: Airway
B: Breathing
C: Circulation

Airway: Make sure the airway is open. Extend the head and neck, open the mouth, and pull the tongue forward.

Breathing: Make sure the dog is breathing. Is the chest rising and falling? Can you feel exhaled air against your cheek? If not, give two rapid breaths through the dog's nose before checking circulation.

Circulation: Check gum color, capillary refill time, and pulse. Gum color should be pink. When you press your thumb on the gum, it should regain its color within two seconds. Check the pulse by feeling either the heartbeat on the left side of the rib crate a couple of inches behind the elbow or the pulse on the inside of the thigh, near the groin.

If your dog has a pulse, but is not breathing, administer artificial respiration.

If your dog does not have a pulse, administer cardiopulmonary resuscitation (CPR).

Artificial Respiration

1. Open the dog's mouth; clear passage of secretions and foreign bodies.

2. Pull the dog's tongue forward.

3. Seal your mouth over the dog's nose and mouth, blow into the dog's nose for two seconds, then release.

4. You should see your dog's chest expand; if not, try blowing with more force, making a tighter seal around the lips, or checking for an obstruction (see following).

5. Repeat at a rate of one breath every four seconds.

6. Stop every minute to monitor breathing and pulse.

7. If air collects in the stomach, push down just behind the rib crate every few minutes.

8. Continue until the dog breathes on its own.

Checking the airway.

Check the pulse at the femoral artery.

Normal Values

Respiration:	10–30 breaths per minute at rest
Pulse:	60–120 beats per minute at rest
Temperature:	101.5–102.5°F (38–39°C)
Capillary refill time:	Less than 2 seconds
Gum color:	Pink (not white, red, bluish, yellowish, or with tiny red spots)
Hydration:	Skin should pop back into position within 3 seconds of being lifted

For obstructions, wrap your hands around the abdomen, behind the rib crate, and compress briskly. Repeat if needed. If the dog loses consciousness, extend the head and neck forward, pull the tongue out fully, and explore the throat for any foreign objects.

If due to drowning, turn dog upside down, holding around its waist, and sway back and forth so that water can run out of his mouth. Then administer mouth-to-nose respiration, with the dog's head positioned lower than its lungs.

For any type of emergency, administer the necessary first aid treatment and seek veterinary help *immediately.* If possible, call the veterinary clinic first so they can be prepared for your arrival. In general, always remember the following:
- ✔ Be calm and reassuring; a calm dog is less likely to go into shock.
- ✔ Move the dog as little and as gently as possible.
- ✔ If the dog is in pain, he may bite. Apply a makeshift muzzle with a bandage or tape. Do not muzzle if the dog is having breathing difficulties.

CPR

1. Place your hands, one on top of the other, on the left side of the chest about 2 inches (5 cm) up from and behind the point of the elbow.
2. Press down quickly and release.
3. Compress at a rate of about 100 times per minute.
4. After every 15 compressions give two breaths through the nose. If you have a partner, the partner can give breaths every two or three compressions.

CPR positioning.

TRAINING FOR STOCK WORK

The sight of a group of animals awakens their driving drive, and it's as though they are transformed back to the western plains.

Aussies like to play and love to love, but everything pales compared to the chance to work stock. Many working ranches rely on their Australian Shepherds day in and day out to gather, drive, and control their sheep or cattle. Other Aussie owners enjoy competing with their dogs at organized herding trials. Many people think of Border Collies when they think of herding dogs, but the Aussie is a somewhat tougher character, more adept at working cattle or uncooperative sheep. Its technique differs from the Border Collie, tending to work closer to the stock and with a higher head carriage.

Despite its strong instincts, even the best Aussie needs guidance and training. The best way for an inexperienced Aussie owner to train a new dog is to work with an experienced herding dog trainer. You will be able to benefit not only from their years of experience, but also their dog-broke stock (see page 80) and herding facilities. With the growing popularity of herding as a pastime rather than strictly as a utilitarian necessity,

finding a herding club or class is becoming increasingly easy. The ASCA or USASA can give you local contacts that can in turn direct you to reputable trainers. You can also search under clubs (performance) at *http://www.akc.org*. If you cannot find anyone to help you, you may have to tackle it on your own.

Preliminary Training

Some trainers suggest letting your young pup grow accustomed to interacting with ducks at a young age. The youngster can practice some rudimentary herding skills, but you must take care that the ducks do not turn the tables on your impressionable puppy! If the pup becomes too rough with the ducks, simply remove him from them without harsh corrections, which could dampen his enthusiasm. Many trainers advocate postponing any work with stock until the dog is 10 to 12 months old. There is plenty of preliminary work to keep both of you busy meanwhile. Some commands are best taught our dog should know *..tay*, and *come*, and *..ill Do"* (or *"OK"*). These ..just as they are for ..nce (see pages 40–43). You may also be able to practice the *steady* command away from stock. The other commands are easier to teach while actually working with stock (although some innovative trainers teach these commands using a toy or ball on the end of a fishing pole-type arrangement). You should practice these commands around all types of distractions except stock; when your dog is finally introduced to stock, he will probably be somewhat out of control and may ignore your commands. This is to be expected and is no cause for you to despair.

Equipment

Once you feel it is time to introduce your Aussie to real stock, you will need:

1. Stock, preferably ducks or sheep.

2. Working pen. For sheep, this is ideally a round or oval pen about 50 to 70 feet (15 to 21 m) in diameter and clear of trees and bushes. Pens for ducks can be smaller.

3. Crook. You can make one out of ½-inch PVC pipe cut to a length of about 5 feet (1.5 m).

Commands

✔ *"Down"*: used to stop the dog. It may later be modified to *"Sit"* or *"Stop."*

✔ *"Stay"*: used to tell the dog to remain in position where it is.

✔ *"Come"*: used to tell the dog to come toward you.

✔ *"Walk Up"*: used to move the dog directly toward the stock.

✔ *"Come Bye"*: used to move the dog in a clockwise direction around the stock.

✔ *"Away to Me"*: used to move the dog in a counterclockwise direction around the stock.

✔ *"Steady"*: used to slow the dog.

✔ *"Get Out"*: used to tell the dog to move away from the stock.

✔ *"Look Back"*: used to tell the dog to look behind it, usually to alert it to a straggling animal.

✔ *"That Will Do"*: used to release the dog from work and call it off the stock.

4. Long line. You can also make this out of thin (about ¼ inch) rope with a bolt snap at one end and a knot at the other, with a total length of about 15 to 20 feet (4.6 to 6.1 m).

Stock

You will want to start with at least five to ten head of stock. Larger stock should be "dog-broke," meaning it is already experienced with being worked by dogs. Dog-broke stock may be available from herding dog trainers or other enthusiasts, or local enthusiasts may be willing

Training the beginning herder to "get out!"

to have their experienced herding dogs practice on your wild bunch. Even so, don't get the first sheep you find. Sheep breeds, like dog breeds, tend to differ in temperament; Dorset crosses are among the easiest to work. Some dogs that are fearful of larger stock may do better with ducks, and ducks are easier to keep. Indian Runners are a good breed of duck for herding. Cattle are best left for later in training, and even then it is best to begin training with calves or goats. Special precautions must be taken with cattle because they can seriously injure your dog. These precautions include making sure your dog is not working between the cattle and a fence that could trap your dog, and removing your dog's collar so it cannot become entangled in a hoof. Cattle are easier to control if they are already moving when your dog approaches them. Remember that if you get your own stock you will need to care for them and provide food, shelter, and veterinary care.

Although we will use sheep in our training examples, keep in mind that you can also use other species, as well as other techniques.

Basic Stock Work

By sprinkling some grain on the ground you can encourage the sheep to stay together in the center of the pen. An assistant is handy for the first few sessions for releasing the dog. Your dog should also drag the long line (attached to a buckle collar) behind for these first sessions.

Introduction to Stock

You have several major goals to reach with your first few sessions. First of all, you want your Aussie to enjoy the experience. You don't want your dog to be scared of the stock, you, or your crook. Most dogs have a tendency to get in too close to the sheep. If this happens, push the dog away, with the crook if necessary, and yell *"Get out!"* Try to use the least force necessary to get the dog away from the sheep. If the dog continues to go at the sheep, position yourself between the sheep and the dog and, as the dog circles, walk in a smaller circle so that you are always between them, pushing the dog out with the crook as necessary. Many pups will race crazily around the sheep, perhaps jumping in and nipping at them. As long as the dog is not hurting the sheep it's usually best to just let him get this initial excitement out of his system. If the dog is really too rough it may be best to postpone training until he is a little older, or accustom the dog to wearing a muzzle and have him wear it while training. If you use too much force you may sour the dog on the whole activity. It is easier to get rambunctious dogs off stock than to encourage timid dogs to approach stock.

The Balance Point

Your second general goal is to help your Aussie learn to find the balance point, which is the point at which the sheep attend to the dog without running from him. Remember that although the instinct to herd sheep is strong in your Aussie, the knowledge of how to herd is not. At first your Aussie will experiment a bit, just as you would if trying to manage a group of sheep. You would find that if you ran headlong into them they would disperse and get out of control. You would find that if you stayed too far away from them they would ignore you and be just as out of your control. At some point you would come to realize that the best way is to approach slowly until you find the balance point; that is, the point at which the sheep are watching you and responding to you without moving away. By moving closer to the sheep from that balance point, they would move away from you, but in a controlled manner. This is what your Aussie must learn, and part of that learning is going to come from trial and error, but he should come to realize that the directions you are giving him are helping him to achieve that balance point and control the sheep.

Driving Versus Gathering

The first specific goal is to eventually have your dog circle the stock. How you achieve this depends on whether your dog naturally tends to drive or gather. Gathering dogs will instinctively tend to position themselves on the opposite side of the flock from you. This means that if you move in a clockwise direction, your dog will do the same in order to keep directly opposite you. By always saying "*Come Bye*" before moving in a clockwise direction, and "*Away to Me*" before moving in a counterclockwise direction, your dog will soon learn the meaning of those commands.

Driving dogs tend to push stock away from the handler and will position themselves between the handler and the sheep. You must block the dog from coming straight into the sheep, either with your arms or the crook as an extension of your arms. The dog will circle out around the sheep in order to avoid you. Be sure to stay between the dog and the sheep, following along slightly behind him in a circle around the sheep. To have the dog turn and circle in the opposite direction, get in front of the dog and walk toward him, giving the appropriate flanking command ("*Come Bye*" or "*Away to Me*"). Use the crook to guide the dog, not hit him. Whichever method you use, it is best if you keep the dog moving at this point. If he stops, then the sheep stop, and this encourages new dogs to run into their midst and scatter them.

Each session should last only about ten minutes. At the end of the session, take the dog by

The correct course of the outrun.

the long line, say "*That will do*," and lead him away from the sheep (not through them). Practice this initial lesson until your dog is circling the sheep and responding to your flanking commands. After a few sessions your dog should be ready for more advanced lessons.

Advanced Stock Work

Fetch: To teach the fetch, position yourself with the sheep between you and the dog and have the dog *down*. Then back away from the sheep so that they move toward you. Call the dog and say "*Walk up.*" The dog should ease toward the sheep. If the dog doesn't move, you can pull him with the long line. If he rushes the sheep, you will have to push him off. If the dog tries to circle the sheep, meet him head on so that he stops and changes direction. It may be easiest to practice with the sheep along one side of the pen so that the dog is less inclined to circle. Walk backwards around the pen, gradually moving away from the fence and walking in smaller circles. Then gradually try walking straight backwards. Once the fetch is mastered, you are ready for the outrun.

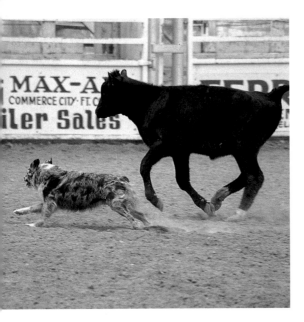

Outrun: To teach the outrun, begin near the sheep with the dog by your side in the *down* position, then give a flanking command in an excited voice. If the dog runs directly to the sheep, run alongside him, forcing him outward. Ideally, the dog should follow a pear-shaped pathway around to the opposite side of the sheep, staying far enough away from the sheep that they do not react. As the dog seems to catch on, gradually back up from the sheep so that the outrun is longer. Eventually, your Aussie should be able to do outruns of 200 to 400 yards (183 to 366 m).

Drive: The drive is essentially the opposite of the fetch, and many dogs have difficulty with it at first because it involves pushing stock away from the handler rather than toward the handler. The best place to teach the drive is on

Herding Terms

✔ **Approach:** how the dog comes toward the stock.
✔ **Balance:** position of the dog that allows him to control the movements of the stock.
✔ **Close-running:** working very near to the stock.
✔ **Crook:** shepherd's staff with a hook on one end.
✔ **Cross-drive:** moving the stock at a right angle to the handler.
✔ **Drive:** move the stock away from the handler.
✔ **Eye:** intense stare by the dog, often while creeping toward the stock.
✔ **Fetch:** bring the stock toward the handler.
✔ **Flanks:** commands telling the dog which direction to circle around the stock.

✔ **Gather:** collect dispersed stock into a compact group.
✔ **Grip:** bite the stock.
✔ **Head:** move in front of the stock to stop its forward progress.
✔ **Heel:** move sheep from behind, usually by heel nipping.
✔ **Lift:** point at which the dog first moves the sheep forward.
✔ **Outrun:** act of running from the handler and around the sheep to their far side.
✔ **Pen:** small enclosure into which stock are driven.
✔ **Shed:** separate one specific animal from the herd.
✔ **Wear:** move the stock toward the handler; also, side-to-side movements of the dog in an effort to group stock.

a dirt road with fences on both sides, but you can improvise a lane with portable construction fencing. With the stock in the lane, place the dog between you and the stock. Give the command "*Walk up.*" Many dogs will attempt to get to the opposite side of the stock so they can move it toward you. If the lane is narrow enough, this will be extremely difficult for the dog to do without causing the sheep to move forward, away from both dog and handler. If the dog tries to get around the side of the stock, *down* him and give the stock a chance to move on before again giving the "*Walk up*" command. This change in direction will confuse many dogs, but eventually your Aussie will get the idea of staying between you and the stock.

Shed: The shed is one of the most difficult, but useful and impressive, of the herding dog's talents. In it, one animal is singled out from the group and kept away from it. To teach it, the herd should be somewhat strung out. The handler then forces a break in the line of animals, causing one animal to become separated. You can also force that break by calling your dog to you through the herd. The herding dog's instinctive reaction is to gather that animal back into the herd, but you must tell it "*This one!*" and then "*Walk up,*" encouraging the dog to approach the single animal. This will take plenty of patience but eventually your Aussie will learn to turn the single animal from the group and hold it there.

Penning: Penning sheep is another task that seems difficult at first. Start by having your Aussie hold sheep to you as you stand alongside a fence. By moving slightly you can cause the sheep to start to bolt in one direction, and your Aussie can practice anticipating their movement and holding them to you. Then stand by a gate and open it toward you, allowing the sheep to go through. *Down* your dog before he can follow them through. In this way he comes to know that you wanted the sheep behind the fence and that he shouldn't rush in and gather them back to you. When your dog is adept at this step, you can set up a gate with only a couple of fence panels on either side, and finally, set up a pen in the middle of the practice area.

Teamwork

Whether training your Aussie for work on the ranch, herding trials, or simply mutual enjoyment, you, too, will most likely find yourself driven. Not only is herding good mental and physical exercise for your Aussie, but the teamwork involved is a wonderful bonding experience. No wonder so many Aussie owners eventually move to the country and find themselves surrounded by sheep!

Training to shed stock from the herd.

ACTIVITIES WITH YOUR AUSTRALIAN SHEPHERD

It's only natural to want to show off the apple of your eye.

It's impossible to own an Aussie without becoming enthralled by the beauty of his deftly controlling a herd of sheep, having your breath taken away by his dazzling agility, or being overwhelmed by his intelligence or the striking picture he makes standing in the field. Proud owners have flaunted their Aussies in herding trials for many years, and more recently have added dog shows, obedience trials, agility competitions, and a bevy of other competitive venues. Aussies have in turn proven to be formidable competitors.

Herding Competitions

Although the true value of a herding dog lies in what he can do on the ranch, many Aussie owners also find enjoyment in herding tests and trials. Tests generally refer to noncompetitive events in which dogs must exhibit a certain level of proficiency to pass; trials usually denote competitive events in which dogs are scored

and placed in relation to one another. Several organizations sponsor tests and trials; although the general requirements are similar, each has slight differences, so you should obtain the official rules from each organization.

The following titles are offered by the different organizations sponsoring herding tests or trials. (Note: The lowercase letter s, c, or d in some titles denotes that the title was earned with either sheep, cattle, or ducks.)

Australian Shepherd Club of America (ASCA)

✔ *Started Trial Dog (STD)*, *Open Trial Dog (OTD)*, and *Advanced Trial Dog (ATD)* represent progressively more demanding trial titles. The *Working Trial Championship (WTCh)* is awarded when the ATD is earned with all three eligible stock species (sheep, cattle, and ducks).

✔ *Post-Advanced Trial Dog (PATD)* requires working stock in a large field.

- *Ranch Trial Dog (RTD)* is awarded based on performance with sheep, goats, or cattle in a ranch setting. It includes pen work, sorting work, chute work, and pasture work, in which the pasture is at least 5 acres.
- *Ranch Dog certification (RD)* is earned with the dog being judged working stock at home. The dog must regularly work stock as an aid to its owner's livelihood. More advanced certifications of Ranch Dog Good (RDG) and Ranch Dog Excellent (RDX) are also awarded.

Request the free Stockdog Rulebook from the ASCA for more detailed information (see page 109 for address).

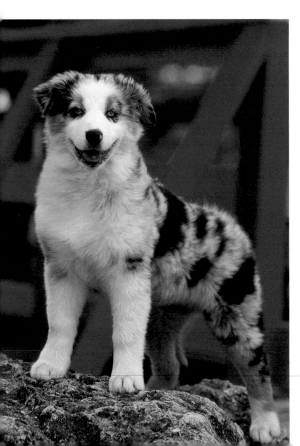

American Kennel Club (AKC)

- *Herding Test (HT)* and *Pre-Trial (PT)* are non-competitive titles based on the display of basic herding instinct and ability.
- *Herding Started (HS)*, *Herding Intermediate (HI)*, and *Herding Excellent (HX)* represent progressively more demanding titles. Three qualifying scores are required for each title.
- *Herding Championships (HCh)* are earned by earning placements in the most advanced level after completing the HX title.

Three types of courses are available: The "A" course requires working stock through obstacles and penning within an arena; the "B" course requires an outrun, lift, fetch, pen, and, for an HX, a shed. The "C" course is performed with larger flocks in more open areas.

Request the herding tests and trials rulebook from the AKC for more detailed information (see page 109 for address).

American Herding Breed Association (AHBA)

Tests:

- *Herding Capability Test (HCT)* consists of a test of basic instinct and of basic stock-moving abilities.
- *Junior Herding Dog Test (JHD)* consists of a simple course ending in a fence-line pen.

To earn these titles requires two qualifying scores using either sheep, goats, ducks, geese, or sometimes cattle.

Trials:

- *Herding Trial Dog trials (HTD)* include three successively more difficult levels (I, II, III), all of which include an outrun, lift, fetch, drive, and pen.
- *Herding Ranch Dog trials (HRD)* include a greater variety of elements and tasks more

like what a working stock dog might actually encounter.

To earn these titles requires two qualifying scores using either sheep, goats, ducks (except for HRD), geese, or cattle. A small initial following the title signifies the species.

✔ *Herding Trial Championship (HTCh)* is awarded after earning ten additional qualifying scores after completing the HTD III or HRD III title.

Obedience Trials

Like all good herding dogs, the Aussie is intelligent and amenable to directions, the two main ingredients of a standout obedience dog. If you don't have access to livestock, you can still exercise your Aussie's mind by training him for competitive obedience. Several organizations, including the ASCA, AKC, and United Kennel Club (UKC), sponsor obedience trials, with progressively more difficult levels. The UKC trials include a few more difficult exercises; the ASCA and AKC trials are similar. The lowest level of AKC or ASCA Companion Dog (CD) requires the dog to:

✔ heel on lead, sitting automatically each time you stop, negotiating right, left, and about turns without guidance from you, and changing to a faster and slower pace.

✔ heel in a figure 8 around two people, still on lead.

✔ stand still off lead 6 feet (1.8 m) away from you and allow a judge to touch him.

✔ do the heeling exercises as before, except off lead.

✔ come to you when called from 20 feet (6.1 m) away, and then return to *heel* position on command.

✔ stay in a sitting position with a group of other dogs, while you are 20 feet (6.1 m) away, for one minute.

✔ stay in a *down* position with the same group, while you are 20 feet (6.1 m) away, for three minutes.

Higher degrees of Companion Dog Excellent (CDX), or Utility Dog (UD) and Utility Dog Excellent (UDX), are a lot more fun and include retrieving, jumping, and hand signal and scent discrimination exercises. The supreme obedience title is the Obedience Trial Champion (OTCH), awarded only to dogs with UDs that outscore many other UD dogs in many, many trials. Very few dogs of any breeds have earned the OTCH degree, but Aussies are among them.

Rally

Rally obedience is more casual that traditional obedience. In rally, you and your dog walk a predetermined course along which numbered signs are placed. Each sign will direct you to have your dog do something, such as sit, circle to the left, do a figure 8, or do an about turn. The exercises and their sequence vary from trial to trial. You can repeat commands, praise your dog, and pretty much act as you would normally except that you can't touch him. Precision is not an important part of rally obedience. Rally has three different degrees of difficulty.

The **Rally Novice (RN)** class is judged with the dog always on leash. It consists of 10 to 15 stations (signs) with no more than five stationary exercises. A dog that passes three times earns the Rally Novice title. Examples of exercises include serpentine weave, down from a walk, moving side-step to the right, circle, and spiral.

The **Rally Advanced (RA)** class is judged with the dog always off leash. It consists of 12 to 17 stations with no more than seven stationary exercises. A dog that passes three times earns the Rally Advanced title. Examples of exercises in addition to the Novice exercises are send over jump, various pivots, and call to heel position.

The **Rally Excellent (RE)** class is judged with the dog always off leash except for the Honor exercise. It consists of 15 to 20 stations with no more than seven stationary exercises. A dog that passes three times earns the Rally Excellent title. Examples of exercises in addition to the Novice exercises are back up three steps, halt-stand-down sequence, and honoring, in which a dog stays in the ring while another dog performs its exercises.

The **Rally Advanced Excellent (RAE)** title is earned by qualifying ten times in both Advanced and Excellent at the same trial.

Dog obedience classes are often sponsored by obedience clubs, and are a must if you plan to compete. They are a valuable source of training advice and encouragement from people who are experienced obedience competitors.

If you enter competition with your Aussie, remember this as your Golden Rule: Companion Dog means just that; being upset at your dog because it made a mistake defeats the purpose of obedience as a way of promoting a harmonious partnership between trainer and dog. Failing a trial is an insignificant event. Never let a ribbon or a few points become more important than a trusting relationship with your companion. Besides, your Aussie will forgive you for the times you mess up!

Tracking Trials

If you enjoy spending misty mornings in the field with your Aussie, you might enjoy tracking. Begin training by walking a simple path and dropping little treats along it. The dog will soon learn that the treats can be discovered simply by following your trail. If your Aussie can't bear to be parted from you, you can also begin training by hiding from him and then allowing him to sniff his way to you. Of course, the actual tracking tests will require considerably more training than this!

A dog can earn the Tracking Dog (TD) title by following a 440- to 500-yard (402- to 457-m) track with three to five turns laid from 30 minutes to 2 hours before. A Tracking Dog Excellent (TDX) title is earned by following an "older" (three to five hours) and longer (800- to 1,000-yard [732- to 914-m]) track with five to seven turns, with some more challenging circumstances, such as the existence of cross tracks laid by another tracklayer about

1½ hours after the first track was laid. The actual track may also cross various types of terrain and obstacles, including plowed land, woods, streams, bridges, and lightly traveled roads.

A dog can earn the Variable Surface Tracking (VST) title by following a three- to five-hour track, 600 to 800 yards (549 to 732 m) long, over a variety of surfaces such as might be normally encountered when tracking in the real world. At least three different surface areas are included, of which at least one must include vegetation and at least two must be devoid of vegetation (for example, sand or concrete). Tracks may even go through buildings, and may be crossed by animal, pedestrian, or vehicular traffic. The Champion Tracker Title is awarded to dogs who earn the TD, TDX, and VST titles. Aussies may not have been bred to use their noses, but they have nonetheless proven themselves more than competent at it.

Agility Trials

Aussies can jump, sprint, climb, balance, and weave with amazing nimbleness, and the sport of agility allows them to hone their skills on an obstacle course. Among the obstacles are open and closed tunnels, elevated walk-over, A-frame, seesaws, weave poles, pause table, and several types of jumps. The jumps can be single bars, double bars, broad, solid, and even a tire. An alternative course type, called Jumpers With Weaves (JWW), just uses the jumps, tunnels, and weaves. If the jumps seem too high for your dog, you can elect to compete in the Preferred class, which has lower jump heights. All of the classes have Novice, Open, and Excellent levels with progressively harder courses and shorter times. Your job is to guide your dog from obstacle to obstacle off lead within a certain time limit. Your dog must pass at each level three times to earn each agility title. The ASCA offers three different class types: Regular, which requires all the obstacles to be cleared in a set time; Gamblers, which is a faster-paced class that also requires the dog to work on its own; and Jumpers, which is a fast-paced competition of jumping. Several levels within the classes are offered, and the ASCA offers a plethora of titles. Other organizations also sponsor trials and award titles.

Veratility

The ASCA awards the Versatility Champion (VCH) and Supreme Versatility Champion (SVCH) to dogs that have earned titles in conformation, obedience, and herding. One of the breed's most versatile and titled Aussies is the amazing SVCH WTCH ASCA/AKC/CKC Ch Beauwood's Rustlin in the Sun ASCA/AKC UDT, RD, HI, RV-N, CKC CD.

nothing like the thrill of winning when you are on the other end of the lead!

At an AKC or ASCA show, each time a judge chooses your dog as the best dog of his sex that is not already a Champion he wins up to five points, depending on how many dogs he defeats. To become an AKC Champion (Ch) your Aussie must win 15 points including two majors (defeating enough dogs to win three to five points at a time); an ASCA championship requires 15 points and three majors. The ASCA also awards the A-Ch title for altered dogs.

Community Service

Aussies are very versatile when it comes to competing successfully in a variety of fields. Some Aussies do even more, and win the hearts of those whose lives they touch.

Search and Rescue

Dogs have been used for finding lost people for decades, but only recently have groups of committed dog owners joined together to train their dogs to be ready to save a life. These dogs are available for local emergencies, and may also be prepared to fly across the country in the cases

Don't Stop There

The world of canine competition has something for everyone! How about freestyle, where dogs and their people dance to music, or flyball, where dogs compete on relay teams to run down a short course with four low jumps, catch a ball, and return? In fact, Aussies are one of the dominating breeds in the sport of flyball. For more information, go to *www.flyballdogs.com*, *www.flyball.org*, or *www.u-fli.com*.

Conformation Shows

The Aussie's build reflects its athletic heritage, and conformation shows judge how well each dog conforms to the physical standard of perfection. As long as your Aussie doesn't have any disqualifying traits (including having been spayed, neutered, lacking two normally descended testicles in males, or other problems described on page 108), he is eligible to compete.

The show Aussie must trot easily about the ring and pose when stopped, and allow a judge to touch him all over without showing resentment or shyness. It helps if your Aussie will "bait," that is, look attentively at a little tidbit or toy. Many local kennel clubs offer handling classes and practice matches. Professional handlers can show your dog for you and probably win more often than you would, but there is of disasters. They may search miles of wilderness for a lost child or tons of rubble for a buried victim. Whereas so many dog training activities seem to have little relevance in society, search and rescue is the exception. Your long hours of training just may save a life. If your Aussie is capable of competing in obedience, agility, and tracking, he has the basics of a search-and-rescue (SAR) dog. These dogs must respond reliably to commands, negotiate precarious footing, follow a trail and locate articles, and, most of all, use air scenting to pinpoint the location of a hidden person. Well-trained dogs can locate a person from a quarter of a mile away, or buried under snow, rubble, or even under water—a tall order that several heroic Aussies and their equally heroic handlers have already filled. A SAR dog is only half of the team; handlers must also be trained. Together the development of a SAR team requires many hours of committed work, hours made worthwhile by grateful tears and saved lives.

Therapy

Aussies excel at many roles, but perhaps one of the most important is that of canine therapist. As more of the population becomes elderly and either unable to care for or keep a pet, the result is particularly sad for lonely people who may have relied on the comfort and companionship of a pet throughout most of their independent years. Studies have shown that pet ownership increases life expectancy and petting animals can lower blood pressure. In recent years nursing home residents have come to look forward to visits by dogs, including many Aussies. These dogs must be meticulously well mannered and well groomed; to be registered as a Certified Therapy Dog a dog must demonstrate that he will act in an obedi-

Hero

A true Aussie hero was a Search and Rescue dog aptly named Ranger (officially Sierra Charm's Mountain Ranger). Ranger was certified in Wilderness, Water, Cadaver, Evidence, and Basic Urban Disaster searches and was sent on over 100 missions. In his career he saved four lives, located three bodies, found a murder weapon, and helped locate a kidnapped child. One of his most memorable finds was a hiker near death who had been lost in the mountains for six days. Ranger was tragically killed in the line of duty, and was buried in a place of honor with 200 people in attendance. As one searcher said: "God must have had one serious search up there; he called the best to help . . . ."

ent, outgoing, gentle manner to strangers. The Aussie combines the perfect blend of attributes for this most vital job: they are outgoing but tractable, and just right for a big hug. They can entertain children and adults alike with their endless ability to perform feats of intelligence. They seem to be in tune with what a particular person most needs, giving a gentle nuzzle to the unsure and a big smile to those in need of cheering up. If you've ever wondered how you could make a difference, consider having your Aussie bring a smile to someone's life.

Service Dogs

Aussies have proven themselves as capable guide dogs for the blind, hearing dogs for the deaf, and all-purpose assistants for the physically challenged. These are not part-time jobs, but you can still lend a hand by being a puppy home for Aussies that may one day open the world to others.

SAFETY AND ACTIVITIES

Aussies are smart and obedient dogs, but even they can act upredictably when the unpredictable occurs.

Most Aussie owners exercise their dogs not by herding, agility, or other organized activities but by sharing time together on a walk or run. With the move of many Aussies to more urban areas, special precautions need to be taken for the safety of your dog. Another dog may attack, or a cat may run underfoot, or the chance to exercise that herding instinct may arise; whatever the reason, the trustworthy dog forgets himself for just a moment—and that's all it takes to run in front of a car. Trust is wonderful, but careless or blind trust is deadly.

Protecting Your Pet

1. Never allow your Aussie to run loose near traffic.

2. Never unhook the leash until you know everything about the area.

3. Watch for poisonous snakes, alligators, or other animals that could attack your dog.

4. Watch for small animals and dogs that your dog could chase.

5. Look out for cliffs, roadways, and drainage culverts.

6. Avoid wilderness areas during hunting season.

Walking and Jogging

Walking the dog on lead is an excellent low-impact exercise for both of you, and is especially good for elderly or recovering dogs. If you pick a regular time of day for your walk you will have your own personal fitness coach goading you off the couch like clockwork. For a walk around the neighborhood, use a choke or martingale collar so that it cannot slip over your Aussie's head, a 6-foot (1.8-m) non-chain leash, or a retractable leash. Retractable leashes are great for walks, but you must be especially vigilant when using them because dogs can still dart out into the path of traffic when on them. Keep an eye out for loose dogs and cats, and hold your dog close around stray animals and passing pedestrians.

Keep up a brisk pace, and gradually work up to longer distances. An Aussie should walk at the very least a mile (1.6 km) daily, and would prefer to walk several miles. Jogging can also be fun for your Aussie, but you must work up to longer distances gradually and avoid hot weather. Dogs can't cool themselves as well as humans can, and heatstroke in jogging dogs has taken the lives of far too many. Check the footpads regularly for abrasions, gravel, tearing, or blistering from hot pavement. In winter, check between the pads for balls of ice, and rinse the feet when returning from walking on rock salt. Finally, never jog, jump, or overexert a puppy. Their bones can be overstressed and damaged. Let a pup run until he's tired, but no more.

Although it's tempting to be lazy and jog your dog beside a bicycle or car, these are risky practices. It's too easy for your dog to see a cat or squirrel and either pull you over or run into your path. If you do elect to try the lazy way out, despite warnings, you must train your dog to understand "*heel*" before starting, and have your dog in *heel* position (except farther out from you) when on the move.

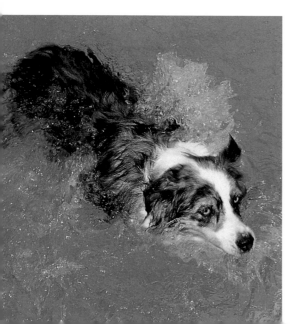

Aussies need exercise, but it must be safe exercise. Do your best to give them this chance, but as the sensible half of the partnership, don't take chances when it comes to safety. Besides, whether walking, jogging, or running, your Aussie will relish most the chance to simply share any adventure, no matter how wild or sedate, with his favorite person—you!

Finding a Lost Dog

Aussies usually stick pretty close to home, but sometimes the unforeseeable happens and you and your dog are suddenly separated. If so, you need to act quickly. Don't rely on the dog's fabled ability to find its way home—yours may not be gifted in this area.

Start your search at the very worst place you could imagine your dog, usually the nearest road, but don't drive so recklessly that you endanger your own dog's life should it run across the road. Next, get pictures of your dog and go door to door. Call the local animal control, police department, and veterinarians. Make up large posters with a picture of your dog or a similar-looking Aussie. Take out an ad in the local paper. Mention a reward, but do not specify an amount.

Identification

Even license tags cannot always ensure your dog's return, because they must be on the dog to be effective. Tattooing your Social Security number or your dog's registration number on the inside of its thigh provides a permanent means of identification; these numbers can be registered with one of the several lost pet recovery agencies. Microchips are available that are placed under the dog's skin with a simple

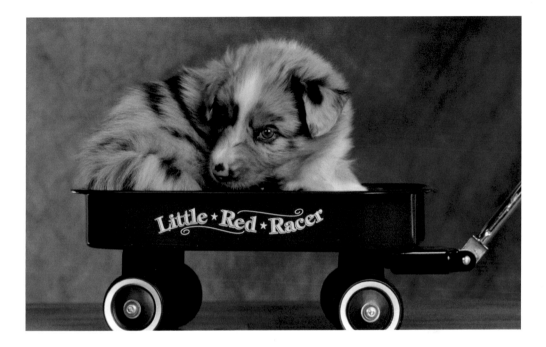

injection. They contain information about the dog and cannot be removed, but require a special scanner (owned by most animal shelters and veterinarians) to be read. You may wish to discuss this option with your veterinarian or local breeders. The best solution is all three: license tag, tattoo, and microchip; of course, the best solution is to never chance getting separated from your companion.

Travel

Aussies make excellent travel companions. A dog gives you a good excuse to stop and enjoy the scenery up close, and maybe even get some exercise along the way. With proper planning, you will find that an Aussie copilot can steer you to destinations you might otherwise have passed.

Without proper planning, sharing your trip with any dog can be a nightmare, as you are turned away from motels, parks, attractions, and beaches. It's no fun trying to sneak a dog into a motel room (Aussies are just a tad too big to fit under your coat; besides, even the mutest Aussie will find plenty to bark at once he discovers you're trying to keep him quiet!). Several books are available listing establishments that accept pets. Call ahead to attractions to see if they have safe boarding arrangements for pets.

The number of establishments that accept pets decreases yearly. You can thank dog owners who seem to think their little Poopsie is above the law, owners who let Poopsie poop on sidewalks, beaches, and playgrounds, bark himself hoarse in the motel room, and leave behind

Items to Pack for Traveling

✔ Heartworm preventive and any other medications, especially antidiarrhea medication
✔ Food and water bowls
✔ Food, dog biscuits, and chewies
✔ Bottled water or water from home; many dogs are very sensitive to changes in water and can develop diarrhea
✔ Flea comb and brush
✔ Moist towelettes, paper towels, and self-rinse shampoo
✔ Bedding
✔ Short and long leashes
✔ Sweater for cold weather
✔ Flashlight for night walks
✔ Plastic baggies or other items for poop disposal
✔ License tags, including a tag indicating where you could be reached while on your trip, or including the address of someone you know will be at home
✔ Health and rabies certificates
✔ Recent color photo in case your Aussie somehow gets lost

wet spots on the carpet and chew marks on the chairs. Miraculously, there still remain some places where pets are welcome. Please do everything you can to convince motel managers that dogs can be civilized guests.

Whether you will be spending your nights at a motel, campground, or even a friend's home, always have your dog on his very best behavior. Ask beforehand if it will be OK for you to bring your Aussie. Have your dog clean and parasite-free. Do not allow your dog to run helter-skelter through the homes of friends. Bring your dog's own clean blanket or bed, or better yet, his crate. Your Aussie will appreciate the familiar place to sleep, and your friends and motel owners will breathe sighs of relief. Even though your dog may be accustomed to sleeping on furniture at home, a proper canine guest stays off the furniture when visiting. Walk your dog (and clean up after him) to make sure no accidents occur

inside. If they do, clean them immediately—don't leave any surprises for your hosts! Changes in water or food, or simply stress, can often result in diarrhea, so be particularly attentive to taking your dog out often.

Never leave your dog unattended in a strange place. The dog's perception is that you have left and forgotten him; he either barks, tries to dig his way out through the doors and windows, or becomes upset and relieves himself on the carpet. Remember that anyone who allows your dog to spend the night is doing so with a certain amount of trepidation.

Car Travel

When in the car your Aussie will want to cuddle in your lap or close by your side, or hang his head out the window for a big whiff of country air. But you are smarter than your Aussie (at least in this matter) and know that he should always ride with the equivalent of a doggy seat belt: the crate. Not only can a crate help prevent accidents by keeping your dog from using your lap as a trampoline, but if there is an accident, a crate can save your dog's life. A crate with a padlocked door can also be useful when you need to leave the dog in the car with the windows down.

Always walk your Aussie on lead when away from home. If frightened or distracted, your dog could become disoriented and lost. The long retractable leads are wonderful for traveling. Keep an eye out for little nature excursions, which are wonderful for refreshing both dog and owner. But always do so with a cautious eye; never risk your or your dog's safety by stopping in totally desolate locales.

Boarding

Sometimes you must leave your dog behind when you travel. Your dog may be more comfortable if an experienced pet-sitter or responsible friend comes to your home and feeds and exercises him regularly. This works best if you have a doggy door.

Your Aussie may be safer (if not quite as contented) if you board him at a kennel. The ideal kennel will be approved by the American Boarding Kennel Association, have climate-controlled accommodations, and will keep your Aussie either indoors or in a combination indoor/outdoor run. Make an unannounced visit to the kennel and ask to see the facilities. While you can't expect spotlessness and a perfumed atmosphere, most runs should be clean and the odor should not be overwhelming. All dogs should have clean water and at least some dogs should have soft bedding. A solid divider should prevent dogs in adjoining runs from direct contact with one another. Strange dogs should not be allowed to mingle. Outside runs should be surrounded by a tall fence for extra security. Good kennels will require proof of immunizations, and an incoming check for fleas. They will allow you to bring toys and bedding, and will administer prescribed medication. They will have arrangements for emergency veterinary care.

Whatever means you choose, always leave emergency numbers and your veterinarian's name. Make arrangements with your veterinarian to treat your dog for any problems that may arise. This means leaving a written agreement stating that you give permission for treatment and accept responsibility for charges.

*You and your Aussie have
a lifetime of experiences
to share.*

Changes in Your Aussie

Always remember the promise you made to yourself and your future puppy before you made the commitment to share your life: to keep your interest in your dog and care for him every day of his life with as much love and enthusiasm as you did the first day he arrived home. Remember, too, that your Aussie will change through the years. The Aussie's high energy and natural athleticism sometimes mislead owners into forgetting that Aussies, like all dogs, get old. One day you will look at your youngster and be shocked to discover his face has silvered and his gait has stiffened. He sleeps longer and more soundly than he did as a youngster, and is slower to get going. He may be less eager to play and more content to lie in the sun. Getting your dog to healthy old age is a worthy accomplishment. Just make sure that you appreciate all the stages along the way.

Every stage of an Aussie's life is his best. Anyone who has had an Aussie for his entire life, would probably assert it is the senior Aussie that is the best. With the wisdom of years, he becomes almost human in his ability to tune into your emotions. The older Aussie, his eyes hazy due to cataracts, his gait stiff, and his face gray, is, in the opinion of many fanciers, the most beautiful of all.

Living with an Older Aussie

Keep your older Aussie relatively active. Physical activity and metabolic rates decrease in older animals, so they require fewer calories to maintain the same weight. Older dogs that are fed the same as when they were young risk becoming obese, and have a greater risk of cardiovascular and joint problems. While Aussies of any age enjoy a soft warm bed, it is a necessity for older ones. Arthritis is a common cause of stiffness and lameness, and can be helped with heat, a soft bed, moderate exercise, and possibly drug therapy.

Introduction of a puppy may be welcome and encourage your dog to play, but if your dog is not used to other dogs, the newcomer will more likely be resented and be a source of irritation. Some older dogs become cranky and less patient, especially with puppies or boister-

Ailments in Older Dogs

Ailment	Common Cause
✔ diarrhea	kidney or liver disease, pancreatitis
✔ coughing	heart disease, tracheal collapse, lung cancer
✔ difficulty eating	periodontal disease, oral tumors
✔ decreased appetite	kidney, liver, or heart disease, pancreatitis, cancer
✔ increased appetite	diabetes, Cushing's syndrome
✔ weight loss	heart, liver, or kidney disease, diabetes, cancer
✔ abdominal distention	heart or kidney disease, Cushing's syndrome, tumor
✔ increased urination	diabetes, kidney or liver disease, cystitis, Cushing's syndrome
✔ limping	arthritis, patellar luxation
✔ nasal discharge	tumor, periodontal disease

ous children. But don't just excuse behavioral changes, especially if sudden, as due to aging. They could be symptoms of pain or disease.

Long trips may be grueling, and boarding in a kennel may be upsetting. The immune system may be less effective, so it is important to shield him from infectious disease, chilling, overheating, and any stressful conditions.

Older dogs may experience hearing or visual loss. Be careful not to startle a dog with impaired senses, as a startled dog could snap in self-defense. The slight haziness that appears in the older dog's pupils is normal and has minimal effect upon vision, but some dogs, especially those with diabetes, may develop cataracts. These can be removed by a veterinary ophthalmologist if they are severe. Dogs with gradual vision loss can cope well as long as they are kept in familiar surroundings and extra safety precautions are followed.

In general, any ailment that an older dog has is magnified in severity compared to the same symptoms in a younger dog. Some of the more common symptoms and their possible cause in older Aussies are listed in the table above.

Vomiting and diarrhea in an old dog can signal many different problems; a small older dog cannot tolerate the dehydration that results from continued vomiting or diarrhea, and you should not let it continue unchecked. The older dog should see his veterinarian at least twice a year. Blood tests can detect early stages of diseases that can benefit from treatment.

Older dogs present a somewhat greater anesthesia risk. Most of this increased risk can be negated, however, by first screening dogs with a complete medical workup.

Odor

Older dogs tend to have a stronger body odor, but they could indicate specific problems, such as periodontal disease, impacted anal sacs, seborrhea, ear infections, or even kidney disease. Like people, dogs lose skin moisture as they age, and though dogs don't have to worry about wrinkles, their skin can become dry and itchy. Regular brushing can help by stimulating oil production.

Special Diets

Although some geriatric dogs are overweight, other Aussies lose weight and may need to eat puppy food to keep the pounds on. A special diet is not required unless they have a particular medical need for it (such as obesity: low calorie; kidney failure: low phosphorus; heart failure: low sodium). This should be prescribed by your veterinarian. Older dogs should be fed several small meals instead of one large meal, and fed on time. Moistening dry food or feeding canned food can help dogs with dental problems. They may enjoy eating while lying down or eating from a raised platform.

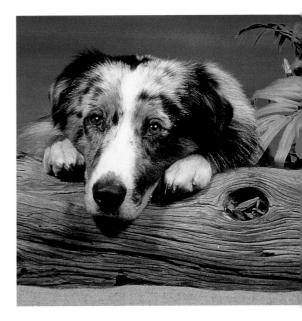

Saying Farewell

If you have an old Aussie, you still must accept that an end will come. Heart disease, kidney failure, and cancer eventually claim most of these senior citizens. Early detection can help delay their effects, but cannot prevent them ultimately. Despite the best of care, a time will come when neither you nor your veterinarian can prevent your cherished pet from succumbing to old age or an incurable illness. Many terminal illnesses make your dog feel very ill, and your desire to keep your friend with you as long as possible may not be the kindest thing for either of you. If your dog no longer eats his dinner or treats, this is a sign that he does not feel well, and you must face the prospect of doing what is best for your beloved friend.

Euthanasia is a difficult and personal decision that no one wishes to make, and that no one can make for you. Ask your veterinarian if there is a reasonable chance of your dog getting better and if it is likely that your dog is suffering. Ask yourself if your dog is getting pleasure out of life and if he enjoys most of his days. When it is time to let go, thank your Aussie for a job well done, and give him the final release.

The Tribute

One of the noblest tributes to a cherished friend is to make a donation to a canine welfare organization such as an Aussie rescue group or health research project.

THE AUSTRALIAN SHEPHERD STANDARD

Australian Shepherds in America are judged under two different but related standards of perfection.

The ASCA, United Kennel Club, and Canadian Kennel Club use the ASCA standard; the AKC uses their own. Both basically seek the same ideal but use different wording. The original standard, the ASCA standard, is used here, with notations of deviation from the AKC standard.

The ASCA Standard

General Appearance: The Australian Shepherd is a well-balanced dog of medium size and bone. He is attentive and animated, showing strength and stamina combined with unusual agility. Slightly longer than tall, he has a coat of moderate length and coarseness with coloring that offers variety and individuality in each specimen. An identifying characteristic is his natural or docked bobtail. In each sex, masculinity or femininity is well-defined.

AKC note: The AKC standard also makes note of the Aussie's strong herding and guarding instincts. It additionally describes the Aussie as lithe, and as being solid and muscular without cloddishness.

Character: The Australian Shepherd is intelligent, primarily a working dog of strong herding and guardian instincts. He is an exceptional companion. He is versatile and easily trained, performing his assigned tasks with great style and enthusiasm. He is reserved with strangers but does not exhibit shyness. Although an aggressive, authoritative worker, viciousness toward people or animals is intolerable.

AKC note: The AKC standard emphasizes that any display of shyness, fear, or aggression is to be severely penalized.

Head: Clean-cut, strong, dry, and in proportion to the body. The top skull is flat to slightly rounded, its length and width each equal to the length of the muzzle, which is in balance and proportioned to the rest if the head. The muzzle tapers slightly to a rounded tip. The stop is moderate but well-defined.

AKC note: The AKC standard states that the muzzle can be slightly shorter than the backskull. Viewed from the side, the topline of the backskull and muzzle form parallel planes divided by the

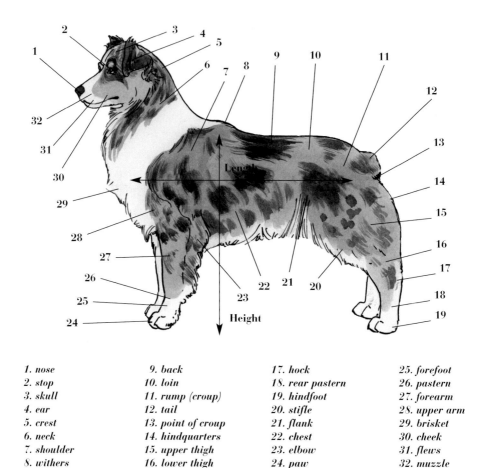

1. nose	9. back	17. hock	25. forefoot
2. stop	10. loin	18. rear pastern	26. pastern
3. skull	11. rump (croup)	19. hindfoot	27. forearm
4. ear	12. tail	20. stifle	28. upper arm
5. crest	13. point of croup	21. flank	29. brisket
6. neck	14. hindquarters	22. chest	30. cheek
7. shoulder	15. upper thigh	23. elbow	31. flews
8. withers	16. lower thigh	24. paw	32. muzzle

stop. The backskull may show a slight occipital protuberance.

Teeth: A full complement of strong, white teeth meet in a scissors bite. An even bite is a fault. Teeth broken or missing by accident are not penalized. Disqualifications: Undershot bites; overshot bites exceeding $1/8$ inch.

AKC note: The AKC standard is more tolerant of a level (even) bite but prefers a scissors bite. It also points out that loss of contact of the upper and lower teeth caused by short center incisors in an otherwise correct mouth should not be considered undershot.

Eyes: Very expressive, showing attentiveness and intelligence. Clear, almond-shaped, and of moderate size, set a little obliquely, neither prominent nor sunken, with pupils dark, well-defined, and perfectly positioned. Color is brown, blue, amber, or any variation or combination including flecks and marbling.

AKC note: The AKC standard does not specify an oblique set, but adds that the expression should be alert and friendly.

Ears: Set on high at the side of the head, triangular and slightly rounded at the tip, of moderate size with length measured by bringing the tip of the ear around to the inner corner of the eye. The ears, at full attention, break slightly forward and over from one-quarter to one-half above the base. Prick ears and hound type ears are severe faults.

AKC note: The AKC standard does not mention a rounded tip and does not specify length.

Neck and Body: The neck is firm, clean, and in proportion to the body. It is of medium length and slightly arched at the crest, settling well into the shoulders. The body is firm and muscular. The topline appears level at a natural four-square stance. The chest is deep and strong with ribs well-sprung. The loin is strong and broad when viewed from the top. The bottom line carries well back with moderate tuck-up. The croup is moderately sloping, the ideal being 30 degrees from the horizontal. Tail is straight, not to exceed 4 inches, natural bobbed or docked.

AKC note: The AKC standard states that the chest should reach to the elbow.

Forequarters: The shoulder blades (scapulae) are long and flat, close set at the withers, approximately two fingers width at a natural stance, and are well laid back at an angle approximately 45 degrees to the ground. The upper arm (humerus) is attached at an approximate right angle to the shoulder line with forelegs dropping straight, perpendicular to the ground. The elbow joint is equidistant from the ground to the withers. The legs are straight and powerful. Pasterns are short, thick, and strong, but still flexible, showing a slight angle when viewed from the side. Feet are oval shaped, compact, with close-knit, well-arched toes. Pads are thick and resilient; nails short and strong. Dewclaws may be removed.

AKC note: The AKC standard specifies that the bone of the foreleg should be strong and oval rather than round.

Hindquarters: Width of hindquarters approximately equal the width of the forequarters at the shoulders. The angulation of the pelvis and the upper thigh (femur) corresponds to the angulation of the shoulder blade and upper arm forming an approximate right angle. Stifles are clearly defined, hock joints moderately bent. The metatarsi are short, perpendicular to the ground, and parallel to each other when viewed from the rear. Feet are oval shaped and compact with close-knit, well-arched toes. Pads are thick and resilient; nails short and strong. Rear dewclaws are removed.

Coat: Of medium texture, straight to slightly wavy, weather resistant, of moderate length with an undercoat. The quantity of undercoat varies with climate. Hair is short and smooth on the head, outside of ears, front of the forelegs, and below the hocks. Backs of the forelegs are moderately feathered; breeches are moderately full. There is a moderate mane and frill, more pronounced in dogs than bitches. Nontypical coats are severe faults.

Color: All colors are strong, clear, and rich. The recognized colors are blue merle, red (liver) merle, solid black, and solid red (liver), all with or without white markings and/or tan (copper) points with no order of preference. The blue merle and black have black pigmentation on the nose, lips, and eye-rims. Red and red merles have liver pigmentation on nose, lips, and eye-rims. Butterfly nose should not be faulted under one year of age. On all colors, the areas surrounding the ears and eyes are dominated by color other than white. The hairline of a white collar does not exceed the point of withers. Disqualifications: other than recognized colors, white body splashes, Dudley nose.

AKC note: The AKC standard more explicitly describes acceptable distribution of white areas.

White is acceptable on the neck (but not to exceed the point of withers at the skin), chest, legs, muzzle, underparts, blaze on head, and white extension from underpart up to 4 inches, measured from a horizontal line at the elbow. In addition, white body splashes are defined as white on the body between withers and tail, on the sides between elbows, and the back of hindquarters. It also states that in merles it is permissible to have small pink spots on the nose, but that these should not exceed 25 percent of the nose in adults.

Gait: Smooth, free, and easy; exhibiting agility of movement with a well-balanced, ground-covering stride. Fore and hind legs move straight and parallel with the center line of the body; as speed increases, the feet, both front and rear, converge toward the center line of gravity of the dog, while the topline remains firm and level.

AKC note: The AKC standard adds that the dog must be agile and able to change direction or alter gait instantly.

Size: Preferred height at the withers for males is 20 to 23 inches; that for females is 18 to 21 inches; however, quality is not to be sacrificed in favor of size.

Disqualifications: Both ASCA and AKC disqualify male dogs that are lacking two normally descended testicles, in addition to those disqualifications mentioned within the body of the standard under color and teeth.

INFORMATION

Organizations
American Kennel Club
www.akc.org

Australian Shepherd Club of America
6091 E. State Highway 21
Bryan, TX 77808-9652
(979) 778-1082
www.asca.org

United States Australian Shepherd Club
9330 N. County Road 15
Ft. Collins, CO 80524
(970) 568-3806
www.australianshepherds.com

Health
Australian Shepherd Health and Genetics
   Institute
www.ashgi.org

Canine Eye Registration Foundation
www.vmdb.org/cerf.html

Canine Health Foundation
www.akcchf.org

Canine Health Information Network
www.caninehealthinfo.org

Double Helix Network
730 E. Weldon Avenue
Fresno, CA 93704-6135
Phone: (559) 264-2685
www.ashgi.org

Epilepsy Resources
www.australianshepherds.org/epilepsy.html

MDR1 Drug Page
www.vetmed.wsu.edu/depts-VCPL/drugs.aspx

Morris Animal Foundation
www.morrisanimalfoundation.org

Orthopedic Foundation for Animals
www.offa.org

University of Pennsylvania Hip Improvement
Program (PennHIP)
www.pennhip.org

Rescue
Aussie Rescue and Placement Hotline
(877) ARPH-779
www.aussierescue.org

Second Time Around Aussie Rescue (STAR)
1-877-RESCUE US (1-877-372-8387)
www.star.org

Pet Finder
www.petfinder.com

Publications
Many books and periodicals can be found listed
at *www.asca.org/Education/Books+and+Videos*

The AS Journal
www.australianshepherds.org/journal.html

Videos
Australian Shepherd Standard
AKC/Video Fulfillment
5580 Centerview Drive, Suite 200
Raleigh, NC 27606-3390
(919) 233-9767

Herding I, II, and III
Canine Training System, Ltd.
7550 W. Radcliffe Avenue
Littleton, CO 80123

Aussie Books and Videos
Hartnagle
13637 Highway 86
Kiowa, CO 80117
(303) 660-6724

INDEX

Cover Photos

Kent Dannen: 4, 12, 13, 36, 81, 82, 84, 89, 91, 92, 98, 107; Jean M. Fogle: 9, 16, 22, 61, 71, 73, 86, 94, 96; Isabelle Francais: 14, 25, 37, 43, 44, 45, 46, 47, 67, 75, 79, 88, 95, 99, 105; Karen Hudson: 78; Paulette Johnson: 2, 6, 7, 11, 19, 24, 26, 29, 30, 33, 38, 41, 49, 50, 53, 60, 62, 72, 87, 97, 100; Pets by Paulette: 5, 52, 56, 59, 69, 101, 103, 104; Shutterstock: 66.

Photo Credits

Isabelle Francais: front cover; Paulette Johnson: inside front cover, inside back cover; Shutterstock: back cover.

About the Author

Caroline Coile is an award-winning author who has written articles about dogs for both scientific and lay publications. She holds a Ph.D. in the field of neuroscience and behavior, with special interests in canine sensory systems, genetics, and behavior. A sighthound owner since 1963, her own dogs have been nationally ranked in conformation, obedience, agility, rally, and field-trial competition.

All inquiries should be addressed to:
Barron's Educational Series, Inc.
250 Wireless Boulevard
Hauppauge, NY 11788
www.barronseduc.com

Library of Congress Catalog Card No. 2009000613

ISBN-13: 978-0-7641-4137-9
ISBN-10: 0-7641-4137-6

Library of Congress Cataloging-in-Publication Data
Coile, D. Caroline.
  Australian shepherds : everything about purchase, care, nutrition, behavior, and training with full-color photographs / D. Caroline Coile.—2nd ed.
    p. cm. — (A complete pet owner's manual)
  Includes bibliographical references and index.
  ISBN-13: 978-0-7641-4137-9
  ISBN-10: 0-7641-4137-6
  1. Australian shepherd dog. I. Title.

SF429.A79C65 2009
636.737—dc22   2009000613

Printed in China
9 8 7 6 5 4

Important Note

This pet owner's guide tells the reader how to buy and care for an Australian Shepherd. The author and the publisher consider it important to point out that the advice given in the book is meant primarily for normally developed puppies from a good breeder—that is, dogs of excellent physical health and good character.

Anyone who adopts a fully grown dog should be aware that the animal has already formed its basic impressions of human beings. The new owner should watch the animal carefully, including its behavior toward humans, and should meet the previous owner. If the dog comes from a shelter, it may be possible to get some information on the dog's background and peculiarities there. There are dogs that, as a result of bad experiences with humans, behave in an unnatural manner or may even bite. Only people who have experience with dogs should take in such animals.

Caution is further advised in the association of children with dogs, and in exercising the dog without a leash.

Even well-behaved and carefully supervised dogs sometimes do damage to someone else's property or cause accidents. It is therefore in the owner's interest to be adequately insured against such eventualities, and we strongly urge all dog owners to purchase a liability policy that covers their dog.